SAP Business One
Complete Self-Assessment Guide

The guidance in this Self-Assessment is based on SAP Business One best practices and standards in business process architecture, design and quality management. The guidance is also based on the professional judgment of the individual collaborators listed in the Acknowledgments.

Notice of rights

You are licensed to use the Self-Assessment contents in your presentations and materials for internal use and customers without asking us - we are here to help.

Trademarks

Copyright © by The Art of Service
http://theartofservice.com
service@theartofservice.com

Table of Contents

About The Art of Service

The Art of Service, Business Process Architects since 2000, is dedicated to helping stakeholders achieve excellence.

Defining, designing, creating, and implementing a process to solve a stakeholders challenge or meet an objective is the most valuable role... In EVERY group, company, organization and department.

Unless you're talking a one-time, single-use project, there should be a process. Whether that process is managed and implemented by humans, AI, or a combination of the two, it needs to be designed by someone with a complex enough perspective to ask the right questions.

Someone capable of asking the right questions and step back and say, 'What are we really trying to accomplish here? And is there a different way to look at it?'

With The Art of Service's Standard Requirements Self-Assessments, we empower people who can do just that — whether their title is marketer, entrepreneur, manager, salesperson, consultant, Business Process Manager, executive assistant, IT Manager, CIO etc... —they are the people who rule the future. They are people who watch the process as it happens, and ask the right questions to make the process work better.

Contact us when you need any support with this Self-Assessment and any help with templates, blue-prints and examples of standard documents you might need:

http://theartofservice.com
service@theartofservice.com

Included Resources - how to access

Included with your purchase of the book is the SAP Business

One Self-Assessment Spreadsheet Dashboard which contains all questions and Self-Assessment areas and auto-generates insights, graphs, and project RACI planning - all with examples to get you started right away.

How? Simply send an email to
access@theartofservice.com
with this books' title in the subject to get the SAP Business One Self Assessment Tool right away.

You will receive the following contents with New and Updated specific criteria:

- The latest quick edition of the book in PDF

- The latest complete edition of the book in PDF, which criteria correspond to the criteria in...

- The Self-Assessment Excel Dashboard, and...

- Example pre-filled Self-Assessment Excel Dashboard to get familiar with results generation

- In-depth specific Checklists covering the topic

- Project management checklists and templates to assist with implementation

INCLUDES LIFETIME SELF ASSESSMENT UPDATES

Every self assessment comes with Lifetime Updates and Lifetime Free Updated Books. Lifetime Updates is an industry-first feature which allows you to receive verified self assessment updates, ensuring you always have the most accurate information at your fingertips.

Get it now- you will be glad you did - do it now, before you forget.

Send an email to **access@theartofservice.com** with this books' title in the subject to get the SAP Business One Self Assessment Tool right away.

Purpose of this Self-Assessment

This Self-Assessment has been developed to improve understanding of the requirements and elements of SAP Business One, based on best practices and standards in business process architecture, design and quality management.

It is designed to allow for a rapid Self-Assessment to determine how closely existing management practices and procedures correspond to the elements of the Self-Assessment.

The criteria of requirements and elements of SAP Business One have been rephrased in the format of a Self-Assessment questionnaire, with a seven-criterion scoring system, as explained in this document.

In this format, even with limited background knowledge of SAP Business One, a manager can quickly review existing operations to determine how they measure up to the standards. This in turn can serve as the starting point of a 'gap analysis' to identify management tools or system elements that might usefully be implemented in the organization to help improve overall performance.

How to use the Self-Assessment

On the following pages are a series of questions to identify to what extent your SAP Business One initiative is complete in comparison to the requirements set in standards.

To facilitate answering the questions, there is a space in front of each question to enter a score on a scale of '1' to '5'.

1 Strongly Disagree

2 Disagree

3 Neutral

4 Agree

5 Strongly Agree

Read the question and rate it with the following in front of mind:

'In my belief,
the answer to this question is clearly defined'.

There are two ways in which you can choose to interpret this statement;
1. how aware are you that the answer to the question is clearly defined
2. for more in-depth analysis you can choose to gather evidence and confirm the answer to the question. This obviously will take more time, most Self-Assessment users opt for the first way to interpret the question and dig deeper later on based on the outcome of the overall Self-Assessment.

A score of '1' would mean that the answer is not clear at all, where a '5' would mean the answer is crystal clear and defined. Leave emtpy when the question is not applicable or you don't want to answer it, you can skip it without affecting your score. Write your score in the space provided.

After you have responded to all the appropriate statements in each section, compute your average score for that section, using the formula provided, and round to the nearest tenth. Then transfer to the corresponding spoke in the SAP Business One Scorecard on the second next page of the Self-Assessment.

Your completed SAP Business One Scorecard will give you a clear presentation of which SAP Business One areas need attention.

SAP Business One Scorecard Example

Example of how the finalized Scorecard can look like:

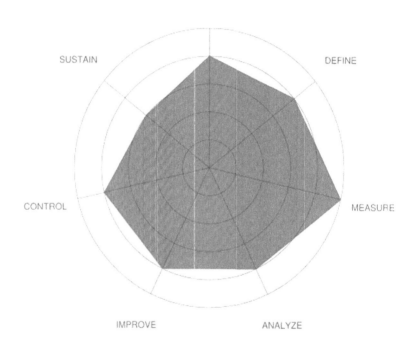

SAP Business One
Scorecard

Your Scores:

BEGINNING OF THE SELF-ASSESSMENT:

CRITERION #1: RECOGNIZE

INTENT: Be aware of the need for change. Recognize that there is an unfavorable variation, problem or symptom.

In my belief, the answer to this question is clearly defined:

5 Strongly Agree

4 Agree

3 Neutral

2 Disagree

1 Strongly Disagree

1. What skills do ERP-Based Implementation Tools leaders need?
<--- Score

2. What problem does an ERP system solve?
<--- Score

3. How do you address the cloud adoption needs of your customers?

<--- Score

4. Have you identified the gaps?
<--- Score

5. To what extent can cloud computing solve problems?
<--- Score

6. What are the main problems or barriers that are delaying progress with your project/ implementation?
<--- Score

7. When and where do ERP-Based Implementation Tools issues surface?
<--- Score

8. How easy is it to add on the type of applications your business needs?
<--- Score

9. What compliance issues should your organization consider?
<--- Score

10. Do you need to consider hybrid implementation?
<--- Score

11. Are there any specific expectations or concerns about the SAP Business One team, SAP Business One itself?
<--- Score

12. What do you need help with?

<--- Score

13. What problems are you facing and how do you consider SAP Business One will circumvent those obstacles?
<--- Score

14. What business problems are you trying to solve with your ERP system?
<--- Score

15. Do you have a need for external users to access the system?
<--- Score

16. As a sponsor, customer or management, how important is it to meet goals, objectives?
<--- Score

17. What kind of infrastructures will be needed for using the cloud ERP system?
<--- Score

18. What is an SAP add on and why do you need one?
<--- Score

19. Does the system have the functionality you need?
<--- Score

20. How are you going to measure success?
<--- Score

21. How much are sponsors, customers, partners, stakeholders involved in SAP Business One? In other

words, what are the risks, if SAP Business One does not deliver successfully?

<--- Score

22. What happens when you need new customization in SAP Business One?

<--- Score

23. Is the product updated frequently enough for your business needs?

<--- Score

24. How do you know you need an ERP system?

<--- Score

25. How are the SAP Business One's objectives aligned to the group's overall stakeholder strategy?

<--- Score

26. Are there any customer satisfaction problems that need to be resolved with the new system?

<--- Score

27. Why do you need models?

<--- Score

28. What would happen if SAP Business One weren't done?

<--- Score

29. What are the challenges and issues of the current implementation?

<--- Score

30. For implementing the ERP system, what kinds of infrastructures are needed?

<--- Score

31. Are there any applications that need to be interfaced with ERP?
<--- Score

32. What is needed by your organizations partners?
<--- Score

33. What business skills and ERP-Based Implementation Tools are needed?
<--- Score

34. What situation(s) led to this SAP Business One Self Assessment?
<--- Score

35. Has your organization identified a project team that will support this project?
<--- Score

36. Where are the gaps that might prevent you from implementing cloud ERP and what do you need to fill them?
<--- Score

37. Do you feel the current system is capable of supporting the needs of the customer?
<--- Score

38. When do you usually issue the Financial Reports?
<--- Score

39. What business problems are you trying to

solve?

<--- Score

40. What does SAP Business One success mean to the stakeholders?

<--- Score

41. How do you maintain flexibility in your ERP system to deal with changing supply chain needs?

<--- Score

42. What issues do you contend that are unique to your particular business?

<--- Score

43. Do you feel you need additional training on the existing system?

<--- Score

44. Which functions need not be available at all times?

<--- Score

45. What kind of infrastructures will be needed for implementing your ERP system?

<--- Score

46. Do you feel you have adequate support to address ERP questions/problems (e.g., User Support Services, service desk)?

<--- Score

47. Do you need to narrow the group of assets further?

<--- Score

48. Who else hopes to benefit from it?
<--- Score

49. What are the stakeholder objectives to be achieved with SAP Business One?
<--- Score

50. What do ERP-Based Implementation Tools need in terms of experience expertise?
<--- Score

51. What happens when the options the system allows just are not good enough for your organizations needs?
<--- Score

52. What skills need to be retained?
<--- Score

53. What are the expected benefits of SAP Business One to the stakeholder?
<--- Score

54. How soon do you need things to stabilise fully after going live in an ERP implementation?
<--- Score

Add up total points for this section:
_ _ _ _ _ = Total points for this section

Divided by: _ _ _ _ _ _ (number of statements answered) = _ _ _ _ _ _
Average score for this section

Transfer your score to the SAP Business One Index at the beginning of the Self-

Assessment.

CRITERION #2: DEFINE:

INTENT: Formulate the stakeholder problem. Define the problem, needs and objectives.

In my belief, the answer to this question is clearly defined:

5 Strongly Agree

4 Agree

3 Neutral

2 Disagree

1 Strongly Disagree

1. What business capabilities do you require to realize your business product?
<--- Score

2. What are the compelling stakeholder reasons for embarking on SAP Business One?
<--- Score

3. Is the current 'as is' process being followed? If not,

what are the discrepancies?

<--- Score

4. Is the team equipped with available and reliable resources?

<--- Score

5. What is scope creep and why is it important to manage during an implementation?

<--- Score

6. Has everyone on the team, including the team leaders, been properly trained?

<--- Score

7. Is a stock take required?

<--- Score

8. What constraints exist that might impact the team?

<--- Score

9. Has a team charter been developed and communicated?

<--- Score

10. What defines your organizations culture?

<--- Score

11. Are the requirements natures high or seasonally variable?

<--- Score

12. Has the direction changed at all during the course of SAP Business One? If so, when did it change and why?

<--- Score

13. Is there a completed SIPOC representation, describing the Suppliers, Inputs, Process, Outputs, and Customers?
<--- Score

14. Does the team have regular meetings?
<--- Score

15. Are team charters developed?
<--- Score

16. Is the team adequately staffed with the desired cross-functionality? If not, what additional resources are available to the team?
<--- Score

17. Is there a critical path to deliver SAP Business One results?
<--- Score

18. Is there regularly 100% attendance at the team meetings? If not, have appointed substitutes attended to preserve cross-functionality and full representation?
<--- Score

19. Are improvement team members fully trained on SAP Business One?
<--- Score

20. Does the system implement and support current regulatory requirements and legal mandates?
<--- Score

21. Is the improvement team aware of the different versions of a process: what they think it is vs. what it actually is vs. what it should be vs. what it could be?
<--- Score

22. How did the SAP Business One manager receive input to the development of a SAP Business One improvement plan and the estimated completion dates/times of each activity?
<--- Score

23. What specifically is the problem? Where does it occur? When does it occur? What is its extent?
<--- Score

24. Is SAP Business One currently on schedule according to the plan?
<--- Score

25. How does it align with your compliance requirements?
<--- Score

26. Is SAP Business One linked to key stakeholder goals and objectives?
<--- Score

27. What is scope creep and why is it important to manage during an ERP implementation?
<--- Score

28. Is the team formed and are team leaders (Coaches and Management Leads) assigned?
<--- Score

29. When is/was the SAP Business One start date?

<--- Score

30. How will the SAP Business One team and the group measure complete success of SAP Business One?
<--- Score

31. Does SAP Business One adapt to your business specific industry requirements?
<--- Score

32. When is the estimated completion date?
<--- Score

33. Has a project plan, Gantt chart, or similar been developed/completed?
<--- Score

34. Is there a SAP Business One management charter, including stakeholder case, problem and goal statements, scope, milestones, roles and responsibilities, communication plan?
<--- Score

35. Are different versions of process maps needed to account for the different types of inputs?
<--- Score

36. Are stakeholder processes mapped?
<--- Score

37. Is the business ERP-Based Implementation Tools goal clearly defined?
<--- Score

38. What would be the goal or target for a SAP

Business One's improvement team?

<--- Score

39. Are there delivery user requirements?

<--- Score

40. What are the boundaries of the scope? What is in bounds and what is not? What is the start point? What is the stop point?

<--- Score

41. Will team members perform SAP Business One work when assigned and in a timely fashion?

<--- Score

42. In case multiple ERP systems are in place; could you account for what functions are supported by the ORACLE, PEOPLESOFT and SAP environments, and are multiple instances of each?

<--- Score

43. Is a fully trained team formed, supported, and committed to work on the SAP Business One improvements?

<--- Score

44. What are your customization requirements?

<--- Score

45. Are customer(s) identified and segmented according to their different needs and requirements?

<--- Score

46. Does the contract require an upfront long-term commitment?

<--- Score

47. Additional support required for go live?

<--- Score

48. What are the dynamics of the communication plan?

<--- Score

49. Have the customer needs been translated into specific, measurable requirements? How?

<--- Score

50. Who are the SAP Business One improvement team members, including Management Leads and Coaches?

<--- Score

51. What customer feedback methods were used to solicit their input?

<--- Score

52. How does the SAP Business One manager ensure against scope creep?

<--- Score

53. What are the Roles and Responsibilities for each team member and its leadership? Where is this documented?

<--- Score

54. Do the problem and goal statements meet the SMART criteria (specific, measurable, attainable, relevant, and time-bound)?

<--- Score

55. How are workflows defined and implemented?

<--- Score

56. Has anyone else (internal or external to the group) attempted to solve this problem or a similar one before? If so, what knowledge can be leveraged from these previous efforts?
<--- Score

57. How do you know if a field has user-defined values?
<--- Score

58. What are the advantages of using a ERP-Based Implementation Tools Business Case?
<--- Score

59. Will team members regularly document their SAP Business One work?
<--- Score

60. What will be the Hardware & Software requirements?
<--- Score

61. How many positions require experience with ERP systems?
<--- Score

62. What is the business use case for integration?
<--- Score

63. How often are the team meetings?
<--- Score

64. What key stakeholder process output measure(s) does SAP Business One leverage and how?

<--- Score

65. Would your department be capable of leading the implementation and training phase of the new system; or would you require substantial outside assistance?
<--- Score

66. How feasible is cloud ERP and where can you find some noteworthy deployment examples?
<--- Score

67. Has the SAP Business One work been fairly and/ or equitably divided and delegated among team members who are qualified and capable to perform the work? Has everyone contributed?
<--- Score

68. How was the 'as is' process map developed, reviewed, verified and validated?
<--- Score

69. Has the improvement team collected the 'voice of the customer' (obtained feedback – qualitative and quantitative)?
<--- Score

70. Has/have the customer(s) been identified?
<--- Score

71. Is the SAP Business One scope manageable?
<--- Score

72. Are key performance indicators defined?
<--- Score

73. Are there different segments of customers?
<--- Score

74. Is someone approving something others already approved (for example, approving capital expenditures that were approved as part of a budget)?
<--- Score

75. What exactly is the required system behavior?
<--- Score

76. What qualities are required of a good ERP-Based Implementation Tools innovator?
<--- Score

77. What predefined alerts are supplied with the system?
<--- Score

78. Purpose: how does your organization define its purpose?
<--- Score

79. If substitutes have been appointed, have they been briefed on the SAP Business One goals and received regular communications as to the progress to date?
<--- Score

80. How do you keep key subject matter experts in the loop?
<--- Score

81. When are meeting minutes sent out? Who is on the distribution list?

<--- Score

82. What critical content must be communicated –
who, what, when, where, and how?
<--- Score

**83. Are there any marketing materials or product
catalogs required?**
<--- Score

84. Are customers identified and high impact areas
defined?
<--- Score

85. What are the rough order estimates on cost
savings/opportunities that SAP Business One brings?
<--- Score

86. How is the team tracking and documenting its
work?
<--- Score

87. Has a high-level 'as is' process map been
completed, verified and validated?
<--- Score

88. How many requirements?
<--- Score

89. How will variation in the actual durations of each
activity be dealt with to ensure that the expected SAP
Business One results are met?
<--- Score

90. Is there a completed, verified, and validated high-
level 'as is' (not 'should be' or 'could be') stakeholder

process map?
<--- Score

91. Is full participation by members in regularly held team meetings guaranteed?
<--- Score

92. Is the team sponsored by a champion or stakeholder leader?
<--- Score

93. Is data collected and displayed to better understand customer(s) critical needs and requirements.
<--- Score

94. Are there any constraints known that bear on the ability to perform SAP Business One work? How is the team addressing them?
<--- Score

95. Why is the rationale or business case important?
<--- Score

Add up total points for this section:
_ _ _ _ _ = Total points for this section

Divided by: _ _ _ _ _ _ (number of statements answered) = _ _ _ _ _ _
Average score for this section

Transfer your score to the SAP Business One Index at the beginning of the Self-Assessment.

CRITERION #3: MEASURE:

INTENT: Gather the correct data.
Measure the current performance and
evolution of the situation.

In my belief, the answer to this
question is clearly defined:

5 Strongly Agree

4 Agree

3 Neutral

2 Disagree

1 Strongly Disagree

1. How do you enable self service reporting and analysis?
<--- Score

2. What tasks do you perform after implementation, because or regardless of the ERP system?
<--- Score

3. Are high impact defects defined and identified in the stakeholder process?
<--- Score

4. Is Process Variation Displayed/Communicated?
<--- Score

5. One common pitfall is the lack of a comprehensive technology strategy that indicates the objectives of the CIM or ERP implementation: low cost or differentiation?
<--- Score

6. What key measures identified indicate the performance of the stakeholder process?
<--- Score

7. What are the areas of ERP-Based Implementation Tools your role focusses on?
<--- Score

8. To which extent does your organization require visibility and analysis of cloud apps?
<--- Score

9. Is data collected on key measures that were identified?
<--- Score

10. What is the estimated cost or desired not to exceed limit for this effort?
<--- Score

11. Are your ERP-Based Implementation Tools under tight cost restrictions?
<--- Score

12. Is there a Performance Baseline?
<--- Score

13. What steps will be needed to pull this organization-wide analysis together?
<--- Score

14. What is your organizations number one priority when implementing ERP?
<--- Score

15. Do you know and understand your priorities?
<--- Score

16. Is long term and short term variability accounted for?
<--- Score

17. Is the research question sufficiently focused?
<--- Score

18. How large is the gap between current performance and the customer-specified (goal) performance?
<--- Score

19. What costs are eliminated with Cloud Hosting?
<--- Score

20. Are you measuring the ERP-Based Implementation Tools impact on your business goals?
<--- Score

21. What is the cost of installation?

<--- Score

22. What data was collected (past, present, future/ongoing)?
<--- Score

23. **What tasks do you do after implementation, because or regardless of the new ERP system?**
<--- Score

24. **Does consideration of cost seem reasonable?**
<--- Score

25. **Are costs in line with estimates?**
<--- Score

26. **How does the added ERP-Based Implementation Tool impact the final outcome?**
<--- Score

27. **How does SAP Business One reflect vendors transactions in the chart of accounts?**
<--- Score

28. **What kinds of cost estimation models are there?**
<--- Score

29. **What are the most important costs inherent in your business impact?**
<--- Score

30. Is data collection planned and executed?
<--- Score

31. **Will a cloud implementation take too much**

time and cause major disruption?
<--- Score

32. What creates the cost savings for cloud infrastructure?
<--- Score

33. With so much focus on the cloud today, what are the pros and cons of cloud, Hybrid, On-Premise, and other delivery models for your organizations ERP solution?
<--- Score

34. Which approach is least costly?
<--- Score

35. What charts has the team used to display the components of variation in the process?
<--- Score

36. What kind of reporting and analytics capabilities are included with SAP Business One?
<--- Score

37. How much should training cost?
<--- Score

38. What impact has the innovation of the ERP product (internet technology and configuration model) on the critical success factors?
<--- Score

39. How can you judge the fit of cost models in reallife cross-organizational ERP settings?
<--- Score

40. What are the long-term cost implications?
<--- Score

41. What factors determine the cost of ERP software?
<--- Score

42. What capabilities should be the focus?
<--- Score

43. Are key measures identified and agreed upon?
<--- Score

44. Are you capitalising too few cloud software implementation costs?
<--- Score

45. How much does it cost to add users?
<--- Score

46. How do you measure success?
<--- Score

47. What are your options to control costs both before and after implementation?
<--- Score

48. Is a solid data collection plan established that includes measurement systems analysis?
<--- Score

49. What has the team done to assure the stability and accuracy of the measurement process?
<--- Score

50. Does the vendor understand the regulations

that will impact your business?
<--- Score

51. What are the potential ERP-Based Implementation Tools impact values?
<--- Score

52. In terms of financial reporting and analysis, is it much clearer?
<--- Score

53. Independent measures or a weighted portfolio of measures?
<--- Score

54. What savings/avoided costs are estimated with re-engineering?
<--- Score

55. Is key measure data collection planned and executed, process variation displayed and communicated and performance baselined?
<--- Score

56. What is the total cost to the business?
<--- Score

57. What capabilities should be the focus of the ERP-Based Implementation Tools?
<--- Score

58. Have you found any 'ground fruit' or 'low-hanging fruit' for immediate remedies to the gap in performance?
<--- Score

59. What costs are in your on premise environment?
<--- Score

60. Although an ERP system can track costs, lean principles do not necessarily take cost accounting into account, should you?
<--- Score

61. What particular quality tools did the team find helpful in establishing measurements?
<--- Score

62. What costs can be reduced with Cloud Hosting?
<--- Score

63. How are the production system and the competitive priorities linked together?
<--- Score

64. Is the information you are receiving consistent with your independent review and analysis?
<--- Score

65. Who should be doing analysis?
<--- Score

66. How can cost estimation models be compared?
<--- Score

67. Who (which unit) has priority of support?
<--- Score

68. What are the opportunities or impacts of the ERP implementation on management accounting changes?

<--- Score

69. Are process variation components displayed/ communicated using suitable charts, graphs, plots?
<--- Score

70. What are the hidden costs of ERP?
<--- Score

71. What are the key input variables? What are the key process variables? What are the key output variables?
<--- Score

72. Was a data collection plan established?
<--- Score

73. What are the agreed upon definitions of the high impact areas, defect(s), unit(s), and opportunities that will figure into the process capability metrics?
<--- Score

74. Do the suppliers ERP-Based Implementation Tools impact process improvement?
<--- Score

75. Who participated in the data collection for measurements?
<--- Score

76. How can the knowledge gain be measured?
<--- Score

77. Does the system provide a chart of accounts?
<--- Score

78. What does ongoing system maintenance cost

your business?
<--- Score

79. What was the cost of the implementation effort to the extent that this can be identified?
<--- Score

Add up total points for this section:
_ _ _ _ _ = Total points for this section

Divided by: _ _ _ _ _ _ (number of statements answered) = _ _ _ _ _ _
Average score for this section

Transfer your score to the SAP Business One Index at the beginning of the Self-Assessment.

CRITERION #4: ANALYZE:

INTENT: Analyze causes, assumptions and hypotheses.

In my belief, the answer to this question is clearly defined:

5 Strongly Agree

4 Agree

3 Neutral

2 Disagree

1 Strongly Disagree

1. How will data be transferred?
<--- Score

2. Is the ERP-Based Implementation Tools approach business driven?
<--- Score

3. Are vendor and customer data recovery responsibilities clearly documented and communicated?

<--- Score

4. What is the process if the software behaves unpredictably?
<--- Score

5. Are losses documented, analyzed, and remedial processes developed to prevent future losses?
<--- Score

6. Which types of risks arise daily due to process errors?
<--- Score

7. Can you use ERP financial data directly from the system without additional manipulation for reporting purposes?
<--- Score

8. ERP extends mrp and mrpii across your organization and takes a process perspective, so how does ERP improve process performance?
<--- Score

9. What data is removed or deactivated?
<--- Score

10. What does the data say about the performance of the stakeholder process?
<--- Score

11. Which stakeholder characteristics are analyzed?
<--- Score

12. Is your content being fully leveraged across

applications, processes and departments?
<--- Score

13. What drives employee experience?
<--- Score

14. How do you inform new staff about SAP processes and strategies?
<--- Score

15. Were Pareto charts (or similar) used to portray the 'heavy hitters' (or key sources of variation)?
<--- Score

16. Which process areas are included in the product?
<--- Score

17. Do you feel knowledgeable with the current systems processes and capabilities?
<--- Score

18. What tools were used to generate the list of possible causes?
<--- Score

19. Is historical information migrated with data from each legacy tool to the proposed tool?
<--- Score

20. How can you support the growth model with processes and resources?
<--- Score

21. Is the gap/opportunity displayed and communicated in financial terms?

<--- Score

22. Do staff have the necessary skills to collect, analyze, and report data?
<--- Score

23. Is data and process analysis, root cause analysis and quantifying the gap/opportunity in place?
<--- Score

24. Are there people or agencies involved that impede the effectiveness and efficiency of the process?
<--- Score

25. Are there people or departments involved that impede the effectiveness and efficiency of the process?
<--- Score

26. Quantity and quality of data: do new data items need to be collected?
<--- Score

27. What conclusions were drawn from the team's data collection and analysis? How did the team reach these conclusions?
<--- Score

28. What did the team gain from developing a sub-process map?
<--- Score

29. If cloud or hosted, where does data reside?
<--- Score

30. What does the implementation process include?
<--- Score

31. What are your organizational processes that will be managed by the ERP?
<--- Score

32. What were the financial benefits resulting from any 'ground fruit or low-hanging fruit' (quick fixes)?
<--- Score

33. Which project management process simplifications are appropriate for your organization and which are not?
<--- Score

34. How will it help your organization to understand and control the process?
<--- Score

35. Are there any end user devices that can download data from the cloud?
<--- Score

36. What are the data conversion requirements from the existing system, if any?
<--- Score

37. What do you currently like about the database system?
<--- Score

38. Does your organization have a Master Data Model available?
<--- Score

39. Are you able to help your customers successfully manage data?

<--- Score

40. Does SAP Business One systematically track and analyze outcomes for accountability and quality improvement?

<--- Score

41. Do you have an adapter to convert the logs of the ERP system to the common log format defined by the Process Mining tool?

<--- Score

42. What are the pros and cons of your current database system?

<--- Score

43. Do you fully understand your as-is condition versus your could-be/should be processes?

<--- Score

44. Were there any improvement opportunities identified from the process analysis?

<--- Score

45. Have changes been properly/adequately analyzed for effect?

<--- Score

46. Data received by the system are accurate and complete?

<--- Score

47. Did any value-added analysis or 'lean thinking'

take place to identify some of the gaps shown on the 'as is' process map?

<--- Score

48. Procedures and processing rules have been followed?

<--- Score

49. Is access to personal data recorded?

<--- Score

50. Have the problem and goal statements been updated to reflect the additional knowledge gained from the analyze phase?

<--- Score

51. Were any designed experiments used to generate additional insight into the data analysis?

<--- Score

52. Have you considered using a supplier portal with your ERP system to connect with your suppliers and streamline the PO communication process?

<--- Score

53. How much data?

<--- Score

54. Is the database mainstream and globally supported?

<--- Score

55. Will it improve the data information quality?

<--- Score

56. Does your organization require data transfering?

<--- Score

57. How will the data be transmitted or disclosed?

<--- Score

58. What is the general quality of the data?

<--- Score

59. Are pertinent alerts monitored, analyzed and distributed to appropriate personnel?

<--- Score

60. How was the detailed process map generated, verified, and validated?

<--- Score

61. What were the crucial 'moments of truth' on the process map?

<--- Score

62. What problems are you facing with your current database system?

<--- Score

63. What are the advantages/ disadvantages of enacting organizational change at the beginning/ end of an ERP implementation process?

<--- Score

64. How do you identify and analyze stakeholders and their interests?

<--- Score

65. Was a detailed process map created to amplify

critical steps of the 'as is' stakeholder process?
<--- Score

66. Do you use a software tool for process modeling?
<--- Score

67. Who is responsible to look after data over the cloud?
<--- Score

68. When is the period end closing process typically done?
<--- Score

69. What quality tools were used to get through the analyze phase?
<--- Score

70. Are duplicate databases being maintained?
<--- Score

71. Are all lightweight and agile project management process steps applicable to your organization?
<--- Score

72. Is availability and accessibility to project data other than your own of benefit to you?
<--- Score

73. Vendor master data correct?
<--- Score

74. How seriously do departments take the choice process?

<--- Score

75. Was a cause-and-effect diagram used to explore the different types of causes (or sources of variation)?
<--- Score

76. What database is required to run the ERP solution?
<--- Score

77. Which data have to be saved for how long in the database?
<--- Score

78. What master data must be entered into every sales document?
<--- Score

79. How will your existing technology stack, designed to support your ERP system, interface with the new data coming from the cloud?
<--- Score

80. Are some strategic orientations more conducive to new process technologies than others?
<--- Score

81. Is the SAP Business One process severely broken such that a re-design is necessary?
<--- Score

82. What else about data clean-up?
<--- Score

83. Is the data subject to regulation?

<--- Score

84. Are there any data conversion requirements?
<--- Score

85. Is the data worth migrating into the new IT business system?
<--- Score

86. What is the cost of poor quality as supported by the team's analysis?
<--- Score

87. Should the time data be determined before or after the start of production?
<--- Score

88. How will data be retrieved from the system?
<--- Score

89. There is more and more data coming in, from your ERP systems, everywhere. What do you need to consider as part of Finances responsibilities?
<--- Score

90. Did any additional data need to be collected?
<--- Score

91. What are your key SAP Business One indicators that you will measure, analyze and track?
<--- Score

92. Have the types of risks that may impact SAP Business One been identified and analyzed?
<--- Score

93. Are gaps between current performance and the goal performance identified?

<--- Score

94. Where does the data come from and who collects it?

<--- Score

95. Does your organization systematically track and analyze outcomes related for accountability and quality improvement?

<--- Score

96. Is the process accessible for change?

<--- Score

97. What tools were used to narrow the list of possible causes?

<--- Score

98. Where does the opportunity lie?

<--- Score

99. How are employees work processes changed with the ERP implementation?

<--- Score

100. Have any additional benefits been identified that will result from closing all or most of the gaps?

<--- Score

101. Have all non-recommended alternatives been analyzed in sufficient detail?

<--- Score

102. What ERP data can be kept on premise and

what can be moved to the cloud?
<--- Score

103. Are you using a shadow system (e.g., database or worksheet used by your code to maintain/track/report) financial data?
<--- Score

104. How do you manage consent to the storage, use or reporting of personal data in SAP Business One?
<--- Score

105. What are the revised rough estimates of the financial savings/opportunity for SAP Business One improvements?
<--- Score

106. How much data will be converted?
<--- Score

107. Is the performance gap determined?
<--- Score

108. Which process areas are included in the ERP-Based Implementation Tools?
<--- Score

109. How well do you know your processes?
<--- Score

110. Are best practices in an ERP system simply a fancy term for process constraints?
<--- Score

111. Have the concerns of stakeholders to help

identify and define potential barriers been obtained and analyzed?

<--- Score

112. What backend database supports this application?

<--- Score

113. How does data get from your ERP system to the portal?

<--- Score

114. Which user role is being given data Accounts Payable Manager access?

<--- Score

115. Does the cloud provide an opportunity to re-architect your systems?

<--- Score

Add up total points for this section:
_ _ _ _ _ = Total points for this section

Divided by: _ _ _ _ _ _ (number of statements answered) = _ _ _ _ _ _
Average score for this section

Transfer your score to the SAP Business One Index at the beginning of the Self-Assessment.

CRITERION #5: IMPROVE:

INTENT: Develop a practical solution. Innovate, establish and test the solution and to measure the results.

In my belief, the answer to this question is clearly defined:

5 Strongly Agree

4 Agree

3 Neutral

2 Disagree

1 Strongly Disagree

1. Is the master contractor providing timesheets or other appropriate documentation to support invoices?
<--- Score

2. What determines user satisfaction in ERP projects: benefits, barriers or risks?
<--- Score

3. Can your organization provide a system landscape document?

<--- Score

4. How could core ERP components help improve business operations at your organization?

<--- Score

5. Many divisions of organizations seek decentralized financial control. How can an ERP system be implemented to ensure local financial decision making and control?

<--- Score

6. Which strategies for developing Business experience are in use today?

<--- Score

7. Are new and improved process ('should be') maps developed?

<--- Score

8. Who would be considered responsible for mapping system roles to end users?

<--- Score

9. How will the team or the process owner(s) monitor the implementation plan to see that it is working as intended?

<--- Score

10. Who is responsible for the final decision for implementation?

<--- Score

11. What were the underlying assumptions on the

cost-benefit analysis?
<--- Score

12. How did the team generate the list of possible solutions?
<--- Score

13. How could erp vendors make it easier for customers to understand licensing models?
<--- Score

14. What tools were used to evaluate the potential solutions?
<--- Score

15. What information is necessary to develop a budget?
<--- Score

16. Does the solution support mobile devices?
<--- Score

17. With ERP, do you think it takes less time to establish a work breakdown structure number (formerly job order number) after receipt and acceptance of a funding document?
<--- Score

18. How easy is it to develop a solution using SAP ERP software?
<--- Score

19. How do you make sure that blueprint documentation represents the actual implementation?
<--- Score

20. Is the optimal solution selected based on testing and analysis?
<--- Score

21. Which ERP modules could help your organization develop new products?
<--- Score

22. To what extent will the solutions you are currently working with be maintained?
<--- Score

23. Is there a small-scale pilot for proposed improvement(s)? What conclusions were drawn from the outcomes of a pilot?
<--- Score

24. How will the group know that the solution worked?
<--- Score

25. How can you extract the selection criteria from the decisions made by the steering team?
<--- Score

26. How should you optimize your investments across the complex landscape of legacy ERP systems and cutting-edge platforms such as IoT?
<--- Score

27. Food for thought: is ERP a universal solution?
<--- Score

28. Are third-party consultants necessary and/ or recommended to implement the solution

successfully?
<--- Score

29. Does the solution provide built in malware detection capability?
<--- Score

30. What information is available in the relationship map?
<--- Score

31. Was a pilot designed for the proposed solution(s)?
<--- Score

32. Does the solution provide advanced visualization for easy investigation of malicious activity?
<--- Score

33. What error proofing will be done to address some of the discrepancies observed in the 'as is' process?
<--- Score

34. Can you develop faster training?
<--- Score

35. Are there any constraints (technical, political, cultural, or otherwise) that would inhibit certain solutions?
<--- Score

36. What risks are likely to occur in the ERP implementation?
<--- Score

37. How have extended ERP components helped

your organization improve its business?
<--- Score

38. Who declares the result?
<--- Score

39. What tools were most useful during the improve phase?
<--- Score

40. Are possible solutions generated and tested?
<--- Score

41. What are the risks of radical innovation?
<--- Score

42. What are the risks associated in implementing cloud ERP?
<--- Score

43. What attendant changes will need to be made to ensure that the solution is successful?
<--- Score

44. What development capability does the SAP Business One partner offer?
<--- Score

45. Which document is used to move items between warehouses?
<--- Score

46. How you can improve your organizations capabilities to use ERP?
<--- Score

47. What communications are necessary to support the implementation of the solution?
<--- Score

48. Where does this fit into the development cycle?
<--- Score

49. Is a contingency plan established?
<--- Score

50. Does the solution include multiwarehouse functionality?
<--- Score

51. What complimentary solutions are included and supported by the local SAP partner?
<--- Score

52. How has SAP improved business activites?
<--- Score

53. Are the best solutions selected?
<--- Score

54. Describe the design of the pilot and what tests were conducted, if any?
<--- Score

55. What does the 'should be' process map/design look like?
<--- Score

56. How could extended ERP components help improve business operations at your organization?
<--- Score

57. Is a solution implementation plan established, including schedule/work breakdown structure, resources, risk management plan, cost/budget, and control plan?
<--- Score

58. Are improved process ('should be') maps modified based on pilot data and analysis?
<--- Score

59. How can you make the specification easy for others to understand?
<--- Score

60. How to develop innovation: Should your organization use in-house, or best of breed technology?
<--- Score

61. Has your organization improved its financial position?
<--- Score

62. How do you manage the risks of the ERP implementation?
<--- Score

63. Can you optimize the value and service levels of your SAP platforms and applications while lowering risk and staying within budget?
<--- Score

64. Is the implementation plan designed?
<--- Score

65. Were any criteria developed to assist the team in

testing and evaluating potential solutions?
<--- Score

66. Is the solution provider local?
<--- Score

67. What can you do to improve the security level?
<--- Score

68. What is the product map?
<--- Score

69. What are the risks of moving to cloud-based ERP and how do you manage them?
<--- Score

70. What measures can be taken to control risk when implementing your projects?
<--- Score

71. How will the solution help the business keep pace with change and thrive?
<--- Score

72. What tool does SAP Business One provide for inventory counting risk assessment?
<--- Score

73. Who will evaluate?
<--- Score

74. What is SAP Business One's impact on utilizing the best solution(s)?
<--- Score

75. How much has your financial/project

management staffing changed as a result of ERP workload changes?
<--- Score

76. Can ERP-Based Implementation Tools solution be delivered in partial increments?
<--- Score

77. Can you save a journal entry as a draft document?
<--- Score

78. If you could make the decision today, would you continue using your current ERP?
<--- Score

79. You know where you are on the solution centric versus business centric scale?
<--- Score

80. What lessons, if any, from a pilot were incorporated into the design of the full-scale solution?
<--- Score

81. How do you know that your organization will be able to implement your technology roadmap?
<--- Score

82. How are capabilities developed over ERP-Based Implementation Tools?
<--- Score

83. What makes an enterprise solution ERP different from other technology offerings?
<--- Score

84. What is the team's contingency plan for potential problems occurring in implementation?
<--- Score

85. Is pilot data collected and analyzed?
<--- Score

86. What techniques are used to evaluate your ERP implementation project?
<--- Score

87. How does the solution remove the key sources of issues discovered in the analyze phase?
<--- Score

88. Why do organizations need common MAPs for ERP?
<--- Score

89. What tools were used to tap into the creativity and encourage 'outside the box' thinking?
<--- Score

90. Is the scope of the research wide enough to provide understanding?
<--- Score

91. What is the implementation plan?
<--- Score

92. What has changed in the solution in the past 3-5 years?
<--- Score

93. How can ERP improve your organizations business performance?

<--- Score

94. Having selected SAP Business One as your product of choice your next decision is which SAP Business One implementation partner should you contract to do the implementation and on-going support?
<--- Score

95. How complicated is the solution to set up and operate?
<--- Score

96. Is there a cost/benefit analysis of optimal solution(s)?
<--- Score

97. Do you have multiple locations and can your manufacturing ERP solution handle them?
<--- Score

98. What factors influence information system integration risks?
<--- Score

Add up total points for this section:
_ _ _ _ _ = Total points for this section

Divided by: _ _ _ _ _ _ (number of statements answered) = _ _ _ _ _ _
Average score for this section

Transfer your score to the SAP Business One Index at the beginning of the Self-Assessment.

CRITERION #6: CONTROL:

INTENT: Implement the practical solution. Maintain the performance and correct possible complications.

In my belief, the answer to this question is clearly defined:

5 Strongly Agree

4 Agree

3 Neutral

2 Disagree

1 Strongly Disagree

1. What changes to accounting standards are taking place and what does that mean for your organization?
<--- Score

2. Are more recent numbers available today on which to base your workplans?
<--- Score

3. Who has responsibilities with respect to determining your organizations strategy and plans for business management solutions and services?
<--- Score

4. Has the improved process and its steps been standardized?
<--- Score

5. What reporting is required (standard SAP Business One reports and custom written reports)?
<--- Score

6. In which areas did you achieve success with process standardization?
<--- Score

7. Does the software follow standard conventions?
<--- Score

8. What is controlled and by whom?
<--- Score

9. What are the critical parameters to watch?
<--- Score

10. How do enterprise resource planning systems affect organization risk?
<--- Score

11. Is new knowledge gained imbedded in the response plan?
<--- Score

12. How will input, process, and output variables be

checked to detect for sub-optimal conditions?
<--- Score

13. Is there a standardized process?
<--- Score

14. What has been the Implementation Tools experience and learning?
<--- Score

15. Is a response plan in place for when the input, process, or output measures indicate an 'out-of-control' condition?
<--- Score

16. Does job training on the documented procedures need to be part of the process team's education and training?
<--- Score

17. Is there a control plan in place for sustaining improvements (short and long-term)?
<--- Score

18. What quality tools were useful in the control phase?
<--- Score

19. Is knowledge gained on process shared and institutionalized?
<--- Score

20. What is the control/monitoring plan?
<--- Score

21. Is there a recommended audit plan for routine

surveillance inspections of SAP Business One's gains?
<--- Score

22. Is there a transfer of ownership and knowledge to process owner and process team tasked with the responsibilities.
<--- Score

23. What will a business ERP-Based Implementation Tools plan address?
<--- Score

24. Does it conform to known standards of encryption?
<--- Score

25. How should you plan to avoid or correct a lack of integration?
<--- Score

26. What is the difference between a warehouse management system wms and an enterprise resource planning ERP system?
<--- Score

27. How do your enterprise resource planning systems affect your organizations risk?
<--- Score

28. What degree of business process standardization do you aim to achieve?
<--- Score

29. What key inputs and outputs are being measured on an ongoing basis?
<--- Score

30. How can enterprise resource planning facilitate organizational transformation?
<--- Score

31. Are you able to learn from your experiences and mistakes to rapidly improve the offering?
<--- Score

32. How will the process owner and team be able to hold the gains?
<--- Score

33. Does a troubleshooting guide exist or is it needed?
<--- Score

34. Does your organization have a business growth road map planned?
<--- Score

35. Who defined the common process standards?
<--- Score

36. Are suggested corrective/restorative actions indicated on the response plan for known causes to problems that might surface?
<--- Score

37. Have new or revised work instructions resulted?
<--- Score

38. What should the next improvement project be that is related to SAP Business One?
<--- Score

39. Have you carefully defined an action plan for

pre-implementation preparation activities?
<--- Score

40. Do you hire a third party to plan and assist with the implementation of the solution?
<--- Score

41. What are the risks to your organization if you fail to create a succession plan?
<--- Score

42. Works with enterprise resources planning (ERP) systems?
<--- Score

43. Should you hire a third party to plan and assist with the implementation of the solution?
<--- Score

44. How do distribution resource planning (DRP) and enterprise resource planning (ERP) differ?
<--- Score

45. Provides ability to integrate to industry standards best of breed tools?
<--- Score

46. What encryption standard is used?
<--- Score

47. What will your business impact plan address?
<--- Score

48. How does getting help from outside experts contribute to your enterprises resource planning success?

<--- Score

49. Is reporting being used or needed?
<--- Score

50. Are documented procedures clear and easy to follow for the operators?
<--- Score

51. Does the response plan contain a definite closed loop continual improvement scheme (e.g., plan-do-check-act)?
<--- Score

52. Are the financial auditors confident in ability to assess risks associated with enterprise resource planning systems?
<--- Score

53. Does the SAP Business One performance meet the customer's requirements?
<--- Score

54. Are there documented procedures?
<--- Score

55. Will the SaaS model imply a standardized solution?
<--- Score

56. Are major enterprise resource planning (ERP) applications in place?
<--- Score

57. What other systems, operations, processes, and infrastructures (hiring practices, staffing, training,

incentives/rewards, metrics/dashboards/scorecards, etc.) need updates, additions, changes, or deletions in order to facilitate knowledge transfer and improvements?

<--- Score

58. How did you learn the ERP implementation business?

<--- Score

59. How might the group capture best practices and lessons learned so as to leverage improvements?

<--- Score

60. Who is the SAP Business One process owner?

<--- Score

61. Does the existing system have a recovery plan?

<--- Score

62. How does culture impact on the implementation of your enterprise resource planning packages?

<--- Score

63. Does a standard report meet your needs?

<--- Score

64. Is there documentation that will support the successful operation of the improvement?

<--- Score

65. Why is it difficult to choose common standards?

<--- Score

66. How do you report from your enterprise resource planning (ERP) system?
<--- Score

67. Are operating procedures consistent?
<--- Score

68. Does it have the necessary controls and segregation of duties in place?
<--- Score

69. How much education do you plan to complete?
<--- Score

70. What other areas of the group might benefit from the SAP Business One team's improvements, knowledge, and learning?
<--- Score

71. How will report readings be checked to effectively monitor performance?
<--- Score

72. What are the current plans for the future development of the new ERP system?
<--- Score

73. Is a response plan established and deployed?
<--- Score

74. Does it provide any form of business learning?
<--- Score

75. Will any special training be provided for results interpretation?
<--- Score

76. Is there a documented and implemented monitoring plan?
<--- Score

77. Are new process steps, standards, and documentation ingrained into normal operations?
<--- Score

78. What process modeling notation/standard do you use?
<--- Score

79. What plans do you have for future developments/implementation?
<--- Score

80. How does securing executive sponsorship contribute to an enterprise resource plannings success?
<--- Score

81. How will the day-to-day responsibilities for monitoring and continual improvement be transferred from the improvement team to the process owner?
<--- Score

82. Control: how much centralization, drill-down visibility?
<--- Score

83. What is the recommended frequency of auditing?
<--- Score

84. How will new or emerging customer needs/

requirements be checked/communicated to orient the process toward meeting the new specifications and continually reducing variation?

<--- Score

85. What have been the benefits and drawbacks of process standardization?

<--- Score

86. How will the process owner verify improvement in present and future sigma levels, process capabilities?

<--- Score

Add up total points for this section:
_ _ _ _ _ = Total points for this section

Divided by: _ _ _ _ _ _ (number of statements answered) = _ _ _ _ _ _
Average score for this section

Transfer your score to the SAP Business One Index at the beginning of the Self-Assessment.

CRITERION #7: SUSTAIN:

INTENT: Retain the benefits.

In my belief, the answer to this question is clearly defined:

5 Strongly Agree

4 Agree

3 Neutral

2 Disagree

1 Strongly Disagree

1. How safe is the cloud?
<--- Score

2. How are members of the ERP-Based Implementation Tools Team selected?
<--- Score

3. How well do you know your code base?
<--- Score

4. What is the response time of the application for

your business?

<--- Score

5. What can your organization do to use the technology to its fullest advantage?

<--- Score

6. How is access to the PII determined?

<--- Score

7. Is it safe to say that the primary reason is to actually enable your organization to grow?

<--- Score

8. Will employees working from home be able to access the system?

<--- Score

9. Is it necessary to integrate your web store with your ERP system?

<--- Score

10. How does multitenancy benefit the customer?

<--- Score

11. What type of training is preferred: Train the Trainer training or end user training?

<--- Score

12. What is your projected date of implementation?

<--- Score

13. When will you get payback from ERP and how much will it be?

<--- Score

14. What factors are accountable in achieving a changeable ERP system?
<--- Score

15. In terms of lost orders or lost sales, in the past, did you encounter any lost order or sale?
<--- Score

16. What type of organization is SAP Business One designed to support?
<--- Score

17. How will the service provider respond to disasters and ensure continued service?
<--- Score

18. How are host systems secured?
<--- Score

19. How difficult is it to upgrade the ERP software?
<--- Score

20. How does on-line training work?
<--- Score

21. What leads to cloud ERP failures?
<--- Score

22. Do you have a qualified implementation consultant?
<--- Score

23. To whom is your organization accountable?
<--- Score

24. What kind of online help features do you have?
<--- Score

25. What are the main benefits of cloud ERP?
<--- Score

26. What is the biggest IT challenge faced by your organization?
<--- Score

27. Are you ready to introduce cloud-based ERP to your organization?
<--- Score

28. What core functional areas are supported by SAP Business One?
<--- Score

29. Does it help you to actually conform to new laws or regulations much easier?
<--- Score

30. Does mass customisation pay?
<--- Score

31. What is the payback?
<--- Score

32. Is it easier with ERP to do timekeeping functions?
<--- Score

33. What it procurement efficiencies have you implemented in your organization?
<--- Score

34. What is the goal of the ERP implementation?
<--- Score

35. Is a resource or capability imperfectly mobile?
<--- Score

36. What are the ways that people experience ERP-Based Implementation Tools stress?
<--- Score

37. What are the responsibilities of the EA function and each EA role?
<--- Score

38. What should your organizations strategy be?
<--- Score

39. How many prior versions of the software does the ERP software publisher organization support?
<--- Score

40. Number of challenges arise from the fact that different groups are meant to use the same model. Should different versions of the model exist, depending on the use?
<--- Score

41. How much to spend on flexibility?
<--- Score

42. What is the upgrade path?
<--- Score

43. Who is the Business ERP-Based Implementation Tools lead?
<--- Score

44. Do you use ERP regularly to perform your job?
<--- Score

45. What will the user experience be after your rollout?
<--- Score

46. What can system users do in the ERP?
<--- Score

47. Is cloud computing compatible with your organizations internal operation and systems?
<--- Score

48. Is there any product available on the minimum level of encryption?
<--- Score

49. How has the role of systems integrators changed over the years?
<--- Score

50. Are all stakeholders shareholders made known that there is an ongoing SAP projects?
<--- Score

51. Do existing organizational procedures regularly impede the efficient, effective and timely performance of duties?
<--- Score

52. When is it possible to delete items?
<--- Score

53. How many ERP-Based Implementation Tools

support business users are expected?
<--- Score

54. What ERP-Based Implementation Tools factors does your business face?
<--- Score

55. Does ERP increase your project management efficiency?
<--- Score

56. How many exemption certificates do you currently manage?
<--- Score

57. Has your organization quantified project-level investments?
<--- Score

58. What is the business criticality of the ERP-Based Implementation Tools?
<--- Score

59. How does it empower managers and leaders to better manage talent?
<--- Score

60. What are the unwritten rules?
<--- Score

61. Basic choice: shared tenant or separate tenants?
<--- Score

62. How does the architect determine what actions have to be performed?

<--- Score

63. What are the challenges to your organization of running a complicated program such as SAP?
<--- Score

64. Have any change orders been executed?
<--- Score

65. How can locally achieved knowledge be captured?
<--- Score

66. What type of contract do you want?
<--- Score

67. How will concurrent usage of the proposed tools licenses be tracked and reported on?
<--- Score

68. Is there any incentive for the users to take up training?
<--- Score

69. What are the approximate number of internal users?
<--- Score

70. What will make your ERP implementation a success for your organization?
<--- Score

71. What really assures Quality?
<--- Score

72. What are the basic software requirements to

run the SAP Business One application?

<--- Score

73. What interval-based models make sense?

<--- Score

74. What will the ERP-Based Implementation Tools team look like?

<--- Score

75. Do you have experienced experts working in the field of ERP and SaaS?

<--- Score

76. How do you choose the right direction and build the right strategy for your organization?

<--- Score

77. What are the gaps in capabilities between legacy and cloud systems?

<--- Score

78. What will your account manager do for you?

<--- Score

79. Best for whom?

<--- Score

80. Is the system deployed for a fixed period of time?

<--- Score

81. What is the purpose of managing customer groups?

<--- Score

82. To what extent do you value the opinion of employees in relation to introducing cloud ERP?
<--- Score

83. What are the ERP-Based Implementation Tools effect on team performance?
<--- Score

84. Which system(s) would you like to integrate your CRM with?
<--- Score

85. From your perspective, what is changing?
<--- Score

86. Does it actually allow your organization to do business more efficiently?
<--- Score

87. Why does this matter to the CIO?
<--- Score

88. What new innovations is the vendor considering?
<--- Score

89. Will user adoption and change management in the cloud be difficult?
<--- Score

90. Are there any other features of cloud ERP systems that you would like to add?
<--- Score

91. How does SAP Business One determine to which sub-period a transaction belongs to?

<--- Score

92. Who will work on your ERP project and what are their backgrounds?
<--- Score

93. Does the workflow include E-signature capabilities?
<--- Score

94. What do customers get?
<--- Score

95. Who will be performing Period-end Activities?
<--- Score

96. How can you create a user?
<--- Score

97. Which product is right for your organization?
<--- Score

98. What are the advantages of using the project plan embedded in SAP Business One?
<--- Score

99. What are the vendors able to offer and deliver reliably with emergence of new delivery models?
<--- Score

100. How does your organization make sure that its ERP investment pays off in increased profitability?
<--- Score

101. How important is sustainability to your

organizations bottom line?

<--- Score

102. How long did it take for your organization to realise the first wave of benefits from the ERP system?

<--- Score

103. What types of reports are produced currently?

<--- Score

104. What are the business benefits of ERP-Based Implementation Tools?

<--- Score

105. When to move to a cloud model?

<--- Score

106. Do other systems share, transmit, or have access to the PII in the system?

<--- Score

107. Do you have the right IT leadership to guide your organization through this transformation?

<--- Score

108. At the end of the day, how powerful is it going to be?

<--- Score

109. To what extent can the blame for a failed ERP software implementation be apportioned?

<--- Score

110. How can asset inventory be tracked?

<--- Score

111. What is the main purpose of each financial report?

<--- Score

112. What are the technologies used to build and support the system?

<--- Score

113. What leading practice would you bring to the project regarding integration?

<--- Score

114. Are you using labor information from ERP?

<--- Score

115. How long does it take for your organization to realise the first wave of benefits from the ERP system?

<--- Score

116. How will it establish a competitive advantage?

<--- Score

117. Which ERP system does your organization use?

<--- Score

118. Which business functions are linked to your ERP systems?

<--- Score

119. How do your ERP-Based Implementation Tools work together?

<--- Score

120. What ERP-Based Implementation Tool or service will which business provide?

<--- Score

121. Are you sure you know what the potential advantages of cloud ERP are?

<--- Score

122. How can disclosures become part of the system of record?

<--- Score

123. How will you account as you go?

<--- Score

124. Do you have enough back-office support to your Implementation partners?

<--- Score

125. What bottlenecks/difficulties arise?

<--- Score

126. System is installed satisfactorily?

<--- Score

127. How many ERP-Based Implementation Tools does your system demand?

<--- Score

128. Do your e-forms support e-signatures?

<--- Score

129. Can psp/tsp methods be applied to the ERP implementation?

<--- Score

130. Do you have regular ERP-Based Implementation Tools meetings with your staff?
<--- Score

131. Which core business functions do you have in the cloud?
<--- Score

132. Can you track project expenses and revenue?
<--- Score

133. Why SAP business one?
<--- Score

134. When do you typically run the period end closing utility?
<--- Score

135. Which objects have a change (history) log?
<--- Score

136. How sensitive to latency is your application?
<--- Score

137. Do you use a specific implementation method?
<--- Score

138. How will this service be managed and quality assured for your organization?
<--- Score

139. What are your goals and aspirations?
<--- Score

140. What are your relationships with the ERP-Based Implementation Tools community?

<--- Score

141. Can you afford to install enterprise software as it was envisioned in the vendors R&D labs?

<--- Score

142. How integral are the ERP-Based Implementation Tools to your business culture?

<--- Score

143. What is the mission of the EA function in your organization?

<--- Score

144. How secure is cloud ERP?

<--- Score

145. What purchasing-related functions of ERP software must be employed and how intensively?

<--- Score

146. How open is vendors application codebase?

<--- Score

147. Big bang or phased implementation?

<--- Score

148. Will the ERP system response time be as fast as it is on premises?

<--- Score

149. Are you using ERP to review project financial transactions?

<--- Score

150. How many of your projects have failed the Delivery Assurance review?

<--- Score

151. How does a lead become a customer?

<--- Score

152. Under what circumstances do you think using an ASP makes sense?

<--- Score

153. What dependencies are present for ERP-Based Implementation Tools functionality?

<--- Score

154. Who can have ERP-Based Implementation Tools administration privileges?

<--- Score

155. Are ERP implementations qualitatively different from other large systems implementations?

<--- Score

156. What if the cloud providers internet goes down?

<--- Score

157. Which applications are your organizations most mission-critical systems?

<--- Score

158. Can you pay bills, keep track of vendors, write checks, and create purchase orders?

<--- Score

159. Will your organization continue to use this decentralized approach?

<--- Score

160. Are you using your current capacity efficiently?

<--- Score

161. What can happen when there is inadequate attention to change management?

<--- Score

162. Is there any decentralization in purchase?

<--- Score

163. What does this mean to the accounting profession?

<--- Score

164. Where can you find information on the tables used in SAP Business One objects?

<--- Score

165. Is contextual help available on a field or a program?

<--- Score

166. How did others do it?

<--- Score

167. How easy is it to add on new applications?

<--- Score

168. If the protocols you adopted are different, is it necessary to do conversion?

<--- Score

169. Are there any vendor implementation fees?
<--- Score

170. Who assigns a particular auditor?
<--- Score

171. What are the biggest challenges your organization will experience on this project?
<--- Score

172. What business outcomes can the ERP-Based Implementation Tools enable?
<--- Score

173. How long has your organization been selling the proposed tool to public sector clients?
<--- Score

174. Are you getting the full benefit?
<--- Score

175. Would a phased approach to the implementation be acceptable?
<--- Score

176. Does the organization provide any ongoing post-go live deployment services?
<--- Score

177. What are the critical system properties?
<--- Score

178. Does size matter for implementation?
<--- Score

179. How are you paying for this?
<--- Score

180. How many ERP-Based Implementation Tools do the business stakeholders have?
<--- Score

181. Who decides?
<--- Score

182. What is your role in dealing with ERP providers and customers who use ERP?
<--- Score

183. How much time does it take to have a completed purchase request approved prior to forwarding it to the Procurement Support Office?
<--- Score

184. How will the SAP Business One team and your organization measure complete success of SAP Business One?
<--- Score

185. What is your strategy?
<--- Score

186. Who is your ERP-Based Implementation Tools team and how is it organized?
<--- Score

187. Is cloud based ERP the right choice for your organization?
<--- Score

188. What are the top 3 financial challenges facing your organization?

<--- Score

189. What are the benefits to your organization from implementing an ERP system?

<--- Score

190. In terms of communication among the different departments, does the system actually facilitate it?

<--- Score

191. When are you looking to complete this ERP project by?

<--- Score

192. What were the reasons for adopting this approach?

<--- Score

193. What are reported challenges in customization of cloud ERP systems?

<--- Score

194. What are the major areas for increasing efficiency in the SAP system?

<--- Score

195. Can you create customized invoices and print, email or convert them to PDF files for your clients?

<--- Score

196. Do you feel you receive adequate reporting from the existing system?

<--- Score

197. Can you see any patterns of an increase or decrease in fraud over the past few years?

<--- Score

198. What major challenges did you or do you see?

<--- Score

199. Technological uncertainty: will the system work as expected?

<--- Score

200. How do you take into account organizational factors with respect to big bang or phased ?

<--- Score

201. How does your organization achieve competitive advantage even if others use the same ERP system?

<--- Score

202. What are the necessary actions to be taken after ERP implementation?

<--- Score

203. How do you view the privileges or policies carried by a job role?

<--- Score

204. Will your employees be able to use it?

<--- Score

205. What factors are accountable for achieving a changeable ERP system?

<--- Score

206. What implementation methodology will be used to implement and support SAP Business One?

<--- Score

207. What do you feel are the largest inadequacies in the current system?

<--- Score

208. Is the cloud the right choice?

<--- Score

209. Which products/services are important?

<--- Score

210. What is included in your support agreement?

<--- Score

211. What are the main Market Entry Mode Strategies?

<--- Score

212. What ERP-Based Implementation Tools do you expect to hold five years from now?

<--- Score

213. Where do you begin the system of governance?

<--- Score

214. Have you built and tested a working finance model?

<--- Score

215. What is an ideal time to implement the application?

<--- Score

216. Do user groups exist for the proposed tool?
<--- Score

217. What if the customer wants to order multiple items?
<--- Score

218. How will it bring about systems innovation, or new ways of doing business?
<--- Score

219. What if business users want more than what they can accomplish with budgets?
<--- Score

220. What factors are key to implementing the ERP successfully?
<--- Score

221. Are you able to build any new business alliances with partners and suppliers?
<--- Score

222. What are the most pressing business objectives today?
<--- Score

223. Are any third party training resources proposed?
<--- Score

224. Which version of which ERP system was initially implemented in your organization?
<--- Score

225. How will software licenses be systematically tracked and reported on while installed in various locations?

<--- Score

226. Will your business opt for SaaS in the next ERP lifecycle?

<--- Score

227. Are the success frameworks appropriate for your ERP implementation?

<--- Score

228. What options do you offer users that do not want to go the cloud?

<--- Score

229. What is your long-term funding strategy?

<--- Score

230. How many users should use the system at the same time?

<--- Score

231. Is the implementation done in a phased/ module-by-module approach?

<--- Score

232. How important is the experience to the user organizations mission?

<--- Score

233. What business goals are driving your cloud ERP search?

<--- Score

234. What would the consequences of noncompliance be?

<--- Score

235. Do you attend any training course during the implementation?

<--- Score

236. Is soa feasible to integration between erp systems and cloud services?

<--- Score

237. To what extent are key projects being delayed to accommodate disinclined individuals?

<--- Score

238. What is the ERP-Based Implementation Tools of theft and/or diversion?

<--- Score

239. What is the purpose of the inventory audit report?

<--- Score

240. How does SAP Business One facilitate the pick and pack process?

<--- Score

241. When is it time to replace your ERP system?

<--- Score

242. What is the business and IT maturity, complexity and regulatory environment?

<--- Score

243. What are the challenges that affect implementation success?
<--- Score

244. What are the Savings with Cloud ERP Software?
<--- Score

245. Do you believe that security is a concern?
<--- Score

246. What have been the outcomes of establishing the EA function?
<--- Score

247. Do you have instructions to guide the user through the system?
<--- Score

248. For the current application do you have any sunset date or agreements with the service partners?
<--- Score

249. Who is working with Mobile Apps?
<--- Score

250. Does the ERP system facilitate change management in its design?
<--- Score

251. Apart from cloud ERP, what other forms of cloud software have you adopted?
<--- Score

252. How do you move your organization towards

Cloud?
<--- Score

253. What functions are not provided?
<--- Score

254. How do you handle global price changes?
<--- Score

255. How do you get your ERP-Based Implementation Tools to rapidly test ideas?
<--- Score

256. Will the SAP system bring about better logistic management, like warehousing?
<--- Score

257. What are the top 3 operational challenges facing your organization?
<--- Score

258. Which do you think is the correct approach?
<--- Score

259. Are copies stored for no apparent reason?
<--- Score

260. What preset conditions can be used in an approval template?
<--- Score

261. What factors are accountable for achieving a changeable outreach?
<--- Score

262. Are the ERP-Based Implementation Tools use

a subject of the training program?
<--- Score

263. How did others get customers to use it?
<--- Score

264. What information is being collected?
<--- Score

265. Services that you could reduce or cut?
<--- Score

266. Where has the code base originated from?
<--- Score

267. If you want to integrate with an outside system, what middleware is supported?
<--- Score

268. What resources or capabilities do organizations use to achieve competitive advantages through ERP-systems?
<--- Score

269. Are you challenging commonly held views or misconceptions on ERP by asking questions such as Is the ERP system valuable?
<--- Score

270. What role does your external accountant play in your business?
<--- Score

271. When are new functions available?
<--- Score

272. Who provides the training?
<--- Score

273. Should you host the application in the cloud or on-premise?
<--- Score

274. What has changed in ERP-Based Implementation Tools in the past 3-5 years?
<--- Score

275. What are the implications of integrating conventional ERP and Cloud services?
<--- Score

276. Is the return on investment from implementation high and preferably immediate?
<--- Score

277. Have rules been formulated for ERP-Based Implementation Tools changes?
<--- Score

278. Does it meet regulatory compliance goals?
<--- Score

279. Do you outsource any activities / functions?
<--- Score

280. Does the system have the capability to do batch scanning and indexing?
<--- Score

281. How can you eliminate errors to begin with?
<--- Score

282. What training has occurred and how effective has it been?

<--- Score

283. How will you create transparency for the complexity of your legacy internal systems?

<--- Score

284. Is cloud ERP really cheaper?

<--- Score

285. Should you use a fully integrated system or implement a best-of-breed strategy?

<--- Score

286. What are your critical activities and milestones?

<--- Score

287. When was certification and accreditation last completed?

<--- Score

288. Should your organization care about social responsibility when implementing ERP?

<--- Score

289. What are the retention periods of PII for this system?

<--- Score

290. What is the role of the SAP Business One Service Manager?

<--- Score

291. Who has access where, when and for how

long?
<--- Score

292. What are the advantages of working with bin locations?
<--- Score

293. Does your SAP business one partner offer local support and if not what costs are involved in supporting your site remotely and how often can you get someone on-site at your premises?
<--- Score

294. Does the proposed tool offer license reporting out of the box?
<--- Score

295. Are you running multiple siloed applications?
<--- Score

296. What are the reasons for adopting cloud ERP systems by your organization?
<--- Score

297. Who are the current users of the system?
<--- Score

298. Does your organization use software or another tool to determine the justification when requesting funding for a project?
<--- Score

299. Who is involved in the implementation of the ERP system project?
<--- Score

300. How is the audit duration determined?
<--- Score

301. What did initiate the ERP implementation in your corporation?
<--- Score

302. When was the last time the interface was reviewed?
<--- Score

303. Do you know what software tools your organizational systems actually want?
<--- Score

304. Why is now the time to switch to SAP Business One?
<--- Score

305. Who are the leaders in the cloud market?
<--- Score

306. Should you work with a specialized or horizontal vendor?
<--- Score

307. Are there multiple distribution centers?
<--- Score

308. Which knowledge service delivery model is in your organizations best interest?
<--- Score

309. What could your business achieve?
<--- Score

310. What are you looking to track as vendor performance?
<--- Score

311. What are the determining factors to a changeability of an information system?
<--- Score

312. Does the ERP-Based Implementation Tool have security authorization (sa)?
<--- Score

313. What is the vision of your organization in regards to growth and expansion?
<--- Score

314. How well does the Vendor Project Manager, Account Manager and Key Personnel present information and address questions?
<--- Score

315. What are the market trends?
<--- Score

316. What options and penalties does the vendor provide if you terminate the service?
<--- Score

317. How do you get your consultant to rapidly test ideas?
<--- Score

318. How does the effort compare to on-premise ERP implementations?
<--- Score

319. Do you feel the current software supports your organizations mission statement?

<--- Score

320. Does it help you to actually conform to new law or regulations much easier?

<--- Score

321. What are the steps involved to ensure cloud ERP implementation success?

<--- Score

322. How are the design deliverables going to be used in the upcoming implementation phase?

<--- Score

323. When is adopting a cloud-based ERP system the right choice?

<--- Score

324. How can the cloud help?

<--- Score

325. What kind of growth are you experiencing?

<--- Score

326. How should the implementation and information environment be designed?

<--- Score

327. What complimentary solutions are included and supported by the local SAP Business One partner?

<--- Score

328. How do you guarantee security and

compliancy?

<--- Score

329. What modeling tool features are most important?

<--- Score

330. Buy, build, or customize?

<--- Score

331. What does ERP do for your organization?

<--- Score

332. How do you align the ERP environment with your current security landscape?

<--- Score

333. How should the governance and organization of cloud computing be set up?

<--- Score

334. What are the reports used for?

<--- Score

335. What percentage of your workloads are run in deployment environments today?

<--- Score

336. Who is your delivery team and how is it organized?

<--- Score

337. How is Splunk Enterprise different?

<--- Score

338. If your organization were to see growth; could

the existing system manage this growth?

<--- Score

339. Who is to assume operations of the hardware/ infrastructure?

<--- Score

340. Are the subsidiaries operationally similar?

<--- Score

341. What is the pace of your growth?

<--- Score

342. Which application features does your organization currently use?

<--- Score

343. Why implement an ERP system?

<--- Score

344. What types of User Licenses are available in SAP Business One?

<--- Score

345. Do you have a implementation of service delivery channel?

<--- Score

346. Are there products from different vendors in the market to implement this?

<--- Score

347. What are the benefits of using SAP Business One?

<--- Score

348. What will make implementation successful?
<--- Score

349. How do you know if the purchase or sales cycle is complete?
<--- Score

350. What role do information systems consultants play in knowledge creation and integration within ERP projects?
<--- Score

351. Is it easier with ERP to do labor or error corrections?
<--- Score

352. Do you have any in inventory?
<--- Score

353. What are you actually integrating?
<--- Score

354. What are the Macro factors affecting business?
<--- Score

355. What type of testing will be done?
<--- Score

356. Are ERP-Based Implementation Tools areas regularly maintained?
<--- Score

357. What type of architecture does SAP Business One use?
<--- Score

358. Is the ERP-Based Implementation Tool easy to deploy and reliable?

<--- Score

359. On the platform layer, what should be considered when integrating?

<--- Score

360. Does running an aging, out-of-date ERP really damage your business?

<--- Score

361. If a customer invested in analytics for SAP Business One, is that investment protected?

<--- Score

362. Which browsers and platforms are employees using?

<--- Score

363. Why adopt now?

<--- Score

364. If the proposed system is cloud based how are upgrades implemented?

<--- Score

365. How can innovation succeed?

<--- Score

366. Which modules of SAP Business One will be implemented?

<--- Score

367. What do you regard as the biggest benefit of

cloud ERP systems?

<--- Score

368. Why Integrate?

<--- Score

369. What are the top three Application Initiatives over the next 12 months ?

<--- Score

370. Which modules of SAP will be implemented?

<--- Score

371. Does your organization already have team or who provides an implementation team?

<--- Score

372. What is your ERP-Based Implementation Tools experience management?

<--- Score

373. What are the main financial reports?

<--- Score

374. How do you provision roles to users?

<--- Score

375. What is the implementation methodology?

<--- Score

376. How does your organization handle exchange rates in the ERP system?

<--- Score

377. Is a single instance of ERP better?

<--- Score

378. Are the ERP-Based Implementation Tools owned?

<--- Score

379. What does someone working with business ERP-Based Implementation Tools do?

<--- Score

380. What kind of deployment will be used?

<--- Score

381. Do you have the bandwidth to support this?

<--- Score

382. Which method of creating reports is right for you?

<--- Score

383. Do you think that this your ERP project has completed or there are potentially more upgrades to it?

<--- Score

384. Does this system maintain information about individuals?

<--- Score

385. Who inside your organization is receiving the benefits of the cloud ERP?

<--- Score

386. Are there unnecessary checks and balances?

<--- Score

387. How to find errors?

<--- Score

388. What type of support is offered?
<--- Score

389. Does the system offer promises to organizations which outweigh limitations?
<--- Score

390. What are the ways to retire a fixed asset in SAP Business One?
<--- Score

391. Are there any further types of undiscovered work?
<--- Score

392. Does the ERP-Based Implementation Tool provide for traceability of changes?
<--- Score

393. Is there a zeitgeist?
<--- Score

394. What types of support can you expect?
<--- Score

Add up total points for this section:
_ _ _ _ _ = Total points for this section

Divided by: _ _ _ _ _ _ (number of statements answered) = _ _ _ _ _ _
Average score for this section

Transfer your score to the SAP Business One Index at the beginning of the Self-

Assessment.

SAP Business One and Managing Projects, Criteria for Project Managers:

1.0 Initiating Process Group: SAP Business One

1. Are you certain deliverables are properly completed and meet quality standards?

2. What are the constraints?

3. How is each deliverable reviewed, verified, and validated?

4. Have the stakeholders identified all individual requirements pertaining to business process?

5. What are the overarching issues of your organization?

6. What do you need to do?

7. Are there resources to maintain and support the outcome of the SAP Business One project?

8. Although the SAP Business One project manager does not directly manage procurement and contracting activities, who does manage procurement and contracting activities in your organization then if not the PM?

9. Does it make any difference if you am successful?

10. Are you properly tracking the progress of the SAP Business One project and communicating the status to stakeholders?

11. Were decisions made in a timely manner?

12. What will be the pressing issues of tomorrow?

13. What input will you be required to provide the SAP Business One project team?

14. Are identified risks being monitored properly, are new risks arising during the SAP Business One project or are foreseen risks occurring?

15. If the risk event occurs, what will you do?

16. Were escalated issues resolved promptly?

17. Will the SAP Business One project meet the client requirements, and will it achieve the business success criteria that justified doing the SAP Business One project in the first place?

18. What is the stake of others in your SAP Business One project?

19. Are stakeholders properly informed about the status of the SAP Business One project?

20. Which six sigma dmaic phase focuses on why and how defects and errors occur?

1.1 Project Charter: SAP Business One

21. Avoid costs, improve service, and/ or comply with a mandate?

22. Why do you manage integration?

23. Why have you chosen the aim you have set forth?

24. Why is a SAP Business One project Charter used?

25. Is it an improvement over existing products?

26. Market – identify products market, including whether it is outside of the objective: what is the purpose of the program or SAP Business One project?

27. How will you learn more about the process or system you are trying to improve?

28. Review the general mission What system will be affected by the improvement efforts?

29. Are there special technology requirements?

30. Pop quiz – which are the same inputs as in the SAP Business One project charter?

31. What outcome, in measureable terms, are you hoping to accomplish?

32. Why is it important?

33. What are the assigned resources?

34. What is in it for you?

35. SAP Business One project deliverables: what is the SAP Business One project going to produce?

36. What is the purpose of the SAP Business One project?

37. Is time of the essence?

38. What are you trying to accomplish?

39. Fit with other Products Compliments – Cannibalizes?

1.2 Stakeholder Register: SAP Business One

40. Who wants to talk about Security?

41. What are the major SAP Business One project milestones requiring communications or providing communications opportunities?

42. What is the power of the stakeholder?

43. Who is managing stakeholder engagement?

44. How big is the gap?

45. Who are the stakeholders?

46. Is your organization ready for change?

47. How will reports be created?

48. How much influence do they have on the SAP Business One project?

49. How should employers make voices heard?

50. What opportunities exist to provide communications?

51. What & Why?

1.3 Stakeholder Analysis Matrix: SAP Business One

52. What is the relationship among stakeholders?

53. Which conditions out of the control of the management are crucial for the achievement of the outputs?

54. Industry or lifestyle trends?

55. What is the issue at stake?

56. Market developments?

57. What are the reimbursement requirements?

58. Effects on core activities, distraction?

59. How to measure the achievement of the Outputs?

60. How do you manage SAP Business One project Risk?

61. Environmental effects?

62. How does the SAP Business One project involve consultations or collaboration with other organizations?

63. Who has been involved in the area (thematic or geographic) in the past?

64. How do rules, behaviors affect stakes?

65. What obstacles does your organization face?

66. Who will be responsible for managing the outcome?

67. What is your organizations competitors doing?

68. Reputation, presence and reach?

69. If the baseline is now, and if its improved it will be better than now?

70. Who will be affected by the work?

71. Why is it important to identify them?

2.0 Planning Process Group: SAP Business One

72. Professionals want to know what is expected from them; what are the deliverables?

73. If action is called for, what form should it take?

74. Why do it SAP Business One projects fail?

75. To what extent have the target population and participants made the activities own, taking an active role in it?

76. Have operating capacities been created and/or reinforced in partners?

77. To what extent are the participating departments coordinating with each other?

78. What types of differentiated effects are resulting from the SAP Business One project and to what extent?

79. What is a Software Development Life Cycle (SDLC)?

80. What is the NEXT thing to do?

81. To what extent has a PMO contributed to raising the quality of the design of the SAP Business One project?

82. You are creating your WBS and find that you keep

decomposing tasks into smaller and smaller units. How can you tell when you are done?

83. Is the duration of the program sufficient to ensure a cycle that will SAP Business One project the sustainability of the interventions?

84. Is the pace of implementing the products of the program ensuring the completeness of the results of the SAP Business One project?

85. Is your organization showing technical capacity and leadership commitment to keep working with the SAP Business One project and to repeat it?

86. How are it SAP Business One projects different?

87. If task x starts two days late, what is the effect on the SAP Business One project end date?

88. How are the principles of aid effectiveness (ownership, alignment, management for development results and mutual responsibility) being applied in the SAP Business One project?

89. When developing the estimates for SAP Business One project phases, you choose to add the individual estimates for the activities that comprise each phase. What type of estimation method are you using?

90. What do they need to know about the SAP Business One project?

91. How should needs be met?

2.1 Project Management Plan: SAP Business One

92. How do you organize the costs in the SAP Business One project management plan?

93. What is the justification?

94. What did not work so well?

95. How can you best help your organization to develop consistent practices in SAP Business One project management planning stages?

96. How do you manage integration?

97. Is there anything you would now do differently on your SAP Business One project based on past experience?

98. Are there any windfall benefits that would accrue to the SAP Business One project sponsor or other parties?

99. Are there any Client staffing expectations?

100. Where does all this information come from?

101. Development trends and opportunities. What if the positive direction and vision of your organization causes expected trends to change?

102. When is the SAP Business One project

management plan created?

103. Is the appropriate plan selected based on your organizations objectives and evaluation criteria expressed in Principles and Guidelines policies?

104. Does the implementation plan have an appropriate division of responsibilities?

105. Will you add a schedule and diagram?

106. Do there need to be organizational changes?

107. What are the assumptions?

108. Why Change?

109. Do the proposed changes from the SAP Business One project include any significant risks to safety?

110. If the SAP Business One project is complex or scope is specialized, do you have appropriate and/or qualified staff available to perform the tasks?

111. Are comparable cost estimates used for comparing, screening and selecting alternative plans, and has a reasonable cost estimate been developed for the recommended plan?

2.2 Scope Management Plan: SAP Business One

112. Assess the expected stability of the scope of this SAP Business One project how likely is it to change, how frequently, and by how much?

113. Are milestone deliverables effectively tracked and compared to SAP Business One project plan?

114. Has the SAP Business One project scope been baselined?

115. The greatest degree of uncertainty is encountered during which phase of the SAP Business One project life cycle?

116. Is there an on-going process in place to monitor SAP Business One project risks?

117. Do you have the reasons why the changes to your organizational systems and capabilities are required?

118. Have all unresolved risks been documented?

119. What are the risks that could significantly affect the scope of the SAP Business One project?

120. Is your organization structure for both tracking & controlling the budget well defined and assigned to a specific individual?

121. Are stakeholders aware and supportive of the principles and practices of modern software estimation?

122. To whom will the deliverables be first presented for inspection and verification?

123. Are the payment terms being followed?

124. Are there procedures in place to effectively manage interdependencies with other SAP Business One projects, systems, Vendors and your organizations work effort?

125. Are metrics used to evaluate and manage Vendors?

126. Are the schedule estimates reasonable given the SAP Business One project?

127. Is it standard practice to formally commit stakeholders to the SAP Business One project via agreements?

128. Materials available for performing the work?

129. Has process improvement efforts been completed before requirements efforts begin?

130. What are the risks that could significantly affect procuring consultant staff for the SAP Business One project?

131. Has the budget been baselined?

2.3 Requirements Management Plan: SAP Business One

132. Describe the process for rejecting the SAP Business One project requirements. Who has the authority to reject SAP Business One project requirements?

133. How will requirements be managed?

134. Will the SAP Business One project requirements become approved in writing?

135. How detailed should the SAP Business One project get?

136. Who will perform the analysis?

137. Do you really need to write this document at all?

138. How knowledgeable is the team in the proposed application area?

139. Who will approve the requirements (and if multiple approvers, in what order)?

140. Will the contractors involved take full responsibility?

141. How will the requirements become prioritized?

142. Is infrastructure setup part of your SAP Business One project?

143. Is the system software (non-operating system) new to the IT SAP Business One project team?

144. Which hardware or software, related to, or as outcome of the SAP Business One project is new to your organization?

145. Is it new or replacing an existing business system or process?

146. Is the user satisfied?

147. Is stakeholder risk tolerance an important factor for the requirements process in this SAP Business One project?

148. How will bidders price evaluations be done, by deliverables, phases, or in a big bang?

149. Who is responsible for monitoring and tracking the SAP Business One project requirements?

150. What information regarding the SAP Business One project requirements will be reported?

151. Should you include sub-activities?

2.4 Requirements Documentation: SAP Business One

152. How much testing do you need to do to prove that your system is safe?

153. Are there any requirements conflicts?

154. How linear / iterative is your Requirements Gathering process (or will it be)?

155. Who provides requirements?

156. If applicable; are there issues linked with the fact that this is an offshore SAP Business One project?

157. How to document system requirements?

158. Where are business rules being captured?

159. What facilities must be supported by the system?

160. Who is interacting with the system?

161. Is the origin of the requirement clearly stated?

162. What if the system wasn t implemented?

163. What is effective documentation?

164. The problem with gathering requirements is right there in the word gathering. What images does it conjure?

165. How does what is being described meet the business need?

166. Validity. does the system provide the functions which best support the customers needs?

167. What is a show stopper in the requirements?

168. What variations exist for a process?

169. What are the potential disadvantages/ advantages?

170. What marketing channels do you want to use: e-mail, letter or sms?

171. Who is involved?

2.5 Requirements Traceability Matrix: SAP Business One

172. What is the WBS?

173. Why do you manage scope?

174. What are the chronologies, contingencies, consequences, criteria?

175. Why use a WBS?

176. How small is small enough?

177. Describe the process for approving requirements so they can be added to the traceability matrix and SAP Business One project work can be performed. Will the SAP Business One project requirements become approved in writing?

178. How do you manage scope?

179. Will you use a Requirements Traceability Matrix?

180. What percentage of SAP Business One projects are producing traceability matrices between requirements and other work products?

181. Do you have a clear understanding of all subcontracts in place?

182. Is there a requirements traceability process in place?

183. How will it affect the stakeholders personally in career?

2.6 Project Scope Statement: SAP Business One

184. Is the plan under configuration management?

185. What should you drop in order to add something new?

186. Is the plan for your organization of the SAP Business One project resources adequate?

187. Are there backup strategies for key members of the SAP Business One project?

188. Is the scope of your SAP Business One project well defined?

189. Is the SAP Business One project manager qualified and experienced in SAP Business One project management?

190. What is the product of this SAP Business One project?

191. Will there be a Change Control Process in place?

192. What is change?

193. What process would you recommend for creating the SAP Business One project scope statement?

194. Is the quality function identified and assigned?

195. Write a brief purpose statement for this SAP Business One project. Include a business justification statement. What is the product of this SAP Business One project?

196. Are there completion/verification criteria defined for each task producing an output?

197. Will tasks be marked complete only after QA has been successfully completed?

198. Do you anticipate new stakeholders joining the SAP Business One project over time?

199. What actions will be taken to mitigate the risk?

200. Is the SAP Business One project organization documented and on file?

201. Are there adequate SAP Business One project control systems?

202. Did your SAP Business One project ask for this?

2.7 Assumption and Constraint Log: SAP Business One

203. Can you perform this task or activity in a more effective manner?

204. After observing execution of process, is it in compliance with the documented Plan?

205. Diagrams and tables are included to account for complex concepts and increase overall readability?

206. Should factors be unpredictable over time?

207. How can constraints be violated?

208. Is the amount of effort justified by the anticipated value of forming a new process?

209. Model-building: what data-analytic strategies are useful when building proportional-hazards models?

210. Are there procedures in place to effectively manage interdependencies with other SAP Business One projects / systems?

211. Are processes for release management of new development from coding and unit testing, to integration testing, to training, and production defined and followed?

212. Is this process still needed?

213. Is staff trained on the software technologies that are being used on the SAP Business One project?

214. What other teams / processes would be impacted by changes to the current process, and how?

215. Does a documented SAP Business One project organizational policy & plan (i.e. governance model) exist?

216. Contradictory information between document sections?

217. Are you meeting your customers expectations consistently?

218. Have adequate resources been provided by management to ensure SAP Business One project success?

219. Is there adequate stakeholder participation for the vetting of requirements definition, changes and management?

220. Is the definition of the SAP Business One project scope clear; what needs to be accomplished?

221. Are there processes in place to ensure internal consistency between the source code components?

222. Do you know what your customers expectations are regarding this process?

2.8 Work Breakdown Structure: SAP Business One

223. Who has to do it?

224. How will you and your SAP Business One project team define the SAP Business One projects scope and work breakdown structure?

225. How many levels?

226. When does it have to be done?

227. Where does it take place?

228. Is it a change in scope?

229. When do you stop?

230. How much detail?

231. Do you need another level?

232. Is it still viable?

233. What has to be done?

234. How far down?

235. How big is a work-package?

236. Is the work breakdown structure (wbs) defined and is the scope of the SAP Business One project clear

with assigned deliverable owners?

237. Can you make it?

238. Why is it useful?

239. Why would you develop a Work Breakdown Structure?

2.9 WBS Dictionary: SAP Business One

240. Are indirect costs charged to the appropriate indirect pools and incurring organization?

241. Is cost performance measurement at the point in time most suitable for the category of material involved, and no earlier than the time of actual receipt of material?

242. What is wrong with this SAP Business One project?

243. Does the contractors system provide unit costs, equivalent unit or lot costs in terms of labor, material, other direct, and indirect costs?

244. Time-phased control account budgets?

245. Are data elements summarized through the functional organizational structure for progressively higher levels of management?

246. Are estimates developed by SAP Business One project personnel coordinated with the already stated responsible for overall management to determine whether required resources will be available according to revised planning?

247. Are the rates for allocating costs from each indirect cost pool to contracts updated as necessary to ensure a realistic monthly allocation of indirect costs without significant year-end adjustments?

248. Performance to date and material commitment?

249. Does the cost accumulation system provide for summarization of indirect costs from the point of allocation to the contract total?

250. Are records maintained to show full accountability for all material purchased for the contract, including the residual inventory?

251. Appropriate work authorization documents which subdivide the contractual effort and responsibilities, within functional organizations?

252. Incurrence of actual indirect costs in excess of budgets, by element of expense?

253. Identify potential or actual overruns and underruns?

254. Budgets assigned to major functional organizations?

255. What went right?

256. Identify potential or actual budget-based and time-based schedule variances?

257. Does the contractor require sufficient detailed planning of control accounts to constrain the application of budget initially allocated for future effort to current effort?

258. Are records maintained to show how management reserves are used?

259. Are estimates of costs at completion generated in a rational, consistent manner?

2.10 Schedule Management Plan: SAP Business One

260. Are multiple estimation methods being employed?

261. Are SAP Business One project team members involved in detailed estimating and scheduling?

262. Were SAP Business One project team members involved in detailed estimating and scheduling?

263. Are there checklists created to determine if all quality processes are followed?

264. Are tasks tracked by hours?

265. Does the schedule have reasonable float?

266. Is a process defined to measure the performance of the schedule management process itself?

267. Are the SAP Business One project team members located locally to the users/stakeholders?

268. Is there an on-going process in place to monitor SAP Business One project risks?

269. Who is responsible for estimating the activity durations?

270. Are enough systems & user personnel assigned to the SAP Business One project?

271. Is current scope of the SAP Business One project substantially different than that originally defined?

272. Is a process for scheduling and reporting defined, including forms and formats?

273. Has the business need been clearly defined?

274. Is pert / critical path or equivalent methodology being used?

275. Is the ims used by all levels of management for SAP Business One project implementation and control?

276. Is stakeholder involvement adequate?

277. Will rolling way planning be used?

278. Does the business case include how the SAP Business One project aligns with your organizations strategic goals & objectives?

2.11 Activity List: SAP Business One

279. How can the SAP Business One project be displayed graphically to better visualize the activities?

280. In what sequence?

281. What is the LF and LS for each activity?

282. What is the total time required to complete the SAP Business One project if no delays occur?

283. Are the required resources available or need to be acquired?

284. What went wrong?

285. When will the work be performed?

286. Who will perform the work?

287. What are the critical bottleneck activities?

288. What are you counting on?

289. What is your organizations history in doing similar activities?

290. How do you determine the late start (LS) for each activity?

291. How difficult will it be to do specific activities on this SAP Business One project?

292. What is the probability the SAP Business One project can be completed in xx weeks?

293. How much slack is available in the SAP Business One project?

294. What went well?

295. What did not go as well?

296. Is there anything planned that does not need to be here?

2.12 Activity Attributes: SAP Business One

297. What is the general pattern here?

298. Can you re-assign any activities to another resource to resolve an over-allocation?

299. Which method produces the more accurate cost assignment?

300. How else could the items be grouped?

301. How many days do you need to complete the work scope with a limit of X number of resources?

302. Activity: what is Missing?

303. Have constraints been applied to the start and finish milestones for the phases?

304. Would you consider either of corresponding activities an outlier?

305. What activity do you think you should spend the most time on?

306. Were there other ways you could have organized the data to achieve similar results?

307. What is missing?

308. How many resources do you need to complete

the work scope within a limit of X number of days?

309. Does your organization of the data change its meaning?

310. Why?

311. Is there a trend during the year?

312. Are the required resources available?

313. Where else does it apply?

2.13 Milestone List: SAP Business One

314. What is the market for your technology, product or service?

315. What are your competitors vulnerabilities?

316. Usps (unique selling points)?

317. Level of the Innovation?

318. Sustaining internal capabilities?

319. Vital contracts and partners?

320. Marketing - reach, distribution, awareness?

321. Describe the concept of the technology, product or service that will be or has been developed. How will it be used?

322. What background experience, skills, and strengths does the team bring to your organization?

323. How difficult will it be to do specific activities on this SAP Business One project?

324. It is to be a narrative text providing the crucial aspects of your SAP Business One project proposal answering what, who, how, when and where?

325. Information and research?

326. What has been done so far?

327. Loss of key staff?

328. How will the milestone be verified?

329. New USPs?

330. Do you foresee any technical risks or developmental challenges?

331. Global influences?

332. Own known vulnerabilities?

2.14 Network Diagram: SAP Business One

333. What job or jobs precede it?

334. Planning: who, how long, what to do?

335. What activity must be completed immediately before this activity can start?

336. What is the completion time?

337. Where do you schedule uncertainty time?

338. What job or jobs could run concurrently?

339. Why must you schedule milestones, such as reviews, throughout the SAP Business One project?

340. What can be done concurrently?

341. Exercise: what is the probability that the SAP Business One project duration will exceed xx weeks?

342. What are the tools?

343. How difficult will it be to do specific activities on this SAP Business One project?

344. Will crashing x weeks return more in benefits than it costs?

345. If x is long, what would be the completion time

if you break x into two parallel parts of y weeks and z weeks?

346. Which type of network diagram allows you to depict four types of dependencies?

347. If the SAP Business One project network diagram cannot change and you have extra personnel resources, what is the BEST thing to do?

348. What are the Major Administrative Issues?

349. What job or jobs follow it?

350. Are the gantt chart and/or network diagram updated periodically and used to assess the overall SAP Business One project timetable?

2.15 Activity Resource Requirements: SAP Business One

351. Do you use tools like decomposition and rolling-wave planning to produce the activity list and other outputs?

352. What are constraints that you might find during the Human Resource Planning process?

353. How do you manage time?

354. How many signatures do you require on a check and does this match what is in your policy and procedures?

355. How do you handle petty cash?

356. Time for overtime?

357. Other support in specific areas?

358. Organizational Applicability?

359. Are there unresolved issues that need to be addressed?

360. Anything else?

361. Which logical relationship does the PDM use most often?

362. What is the Work Plan Standard?

363. When does monitoring begin?

364. Why do you do that?

2.16 Resource Breakdown Structure: SAP Business One

365. Who delivers the information?

366. Who will be used as a SAP Business One project team member?

367. What is SAP Business One project communication management?

368. Is predictive resource analysis being done?

369. What is the number one predictor of a groups productivity?

370. Why is this important?

371. Which resource planning tool provides information on resource responsibility and accountability?

372. Why time management?

373. Why do you do it?

374. What defines a successful SAP Business One project?

375. How should the information be delivered?

376. Who is allowed to perform which functions?

377. What are the requirements for resource data?

378. What is the difference between % Complete and % work?

379. Which resources should be in the resource pool?

2.17 Activity Duration Estimates: SAP Business One

380. Is the SAP Business One project performing better or worse than planned?

381. Write a oneto two-page paper describing your dream team for this SAP Business One project. What type of people would you want on your team?

382. What is the BEST thing for the SAP Business One project manager to do?

383. Do your results resemble a normal distribution?

384. What should be done NEXT?

385. Which tips for taking the PMP exam do you think would be most helpful for you?

386. Are the causes of all variances identified?

387. Describe SAP Business One project integration management in your own words. How does SAP Business One project integration management relate to the SAP Business One project life cycle, stakeholders, and the other SAP Business One project management knowledge areas?

388. Are performance reviews conducted regularly to assess the status of SAP Business One projects?

389. Does a process exist to determine the potential

loss or gain if risk events occur?

390. What is earned value?

391. Consider the changes in the job market for information technology workers. How does the job market and current state of the economy affect human resource management?

392. How many different communications channels does a SAP Business One project team with six people have?

393. Is risk identification completed regularly throughout the SAP Business One project?

394. Are operational definitions created to identify quality measurement criteria for specific activities?

395. After changes are approved are SAP Business One project documents updated and distributed?

396. What are the main types of contracts if you do decide to outsource?

397. What questions do you have about the sample documents provided?

398. Calculate the expected duration for an activity that has a most likely time of 3, a pessimistic time of 10, and a optimiztic time of 2?

2.18 Duration Estimating Worksheet: SAP Business One

399. What info is needed?

400. When, then?

401. Is a construction detail attached (to aid in explanation)?

402. What is next?

403. Science = process: remember the scientific method?

404. Value pocket identification & quantification what are value pockets?

405. How should ongoing costs be monitored to try to keep the SAP Business One project within budget?

406. Small or large SAP Business One project?

407. What utility impacts are there?

408. What is an Average SAP Business One project?

409. Does the SAP Business One project provide innovative ways for stakeholders to overcome obstacles or deliver better outcomes?

410. When do the individual activities need to start and finish?

411. Why estimate costs?

412. Do any colleagues have experience with your organization and/or RFPs?

413. When does your organization expect to be able to complete it?

414. For other activities, how much delay can be tolerated?

415. Define the work as completely as possible. What work will be included in the SAP Business One project?

416. What questions do you have?

2.19 Project Schedule: SAP Business One

417. Eliminate unnecessary activities. Are there activities that came from a template or previous SAP Business One project that are not applicable on this phase of this SAP Business One project?

418. What documents, if any, will the subcontractor provide (eg SAP Business One project schedule, quality plan etc)?

419. Was the SAP Business One project schedule reviewed by all stakeholders and formally accepted?

420. If you can not fix it, how do you do it differently?

421. What is SAP Business One project management?

422. How effectively were issues able to be resolved without impacting the SAP Business One project Schedule or Budget?

423. Are you working on the right risks?

424. Why do you need to manage SAP Business One project Risk?

425. Is infrastructure setup part of your SAP Business One project?

426. How does a SAP Business One project get to be a year late ?

427. Is the structure for tracking the SAP Business One project schedule well defined and assigned to a specific individual?

428. How can you address that situation?

429. Are procedures defined by which the SAP Business One project schedule may be changed?

430. How do you use schedules?

431. Are the original SAP Business One project schedule and budget realistic?

432. Your SAP Business One project management plan results in a SAP Business One project schedule that is too long. If the SAP Business One project network diagram cannot change and you have extra personnel resources, what is the BEST thing to do?

433. The wbs is developed as part of a joint planning session. and how do you know that youhave done this right?

434. Did the SAP Business One project come in under budget?

2.20 Cost Management Plan: SAP Business One

435. What is an Acceptance Management Process?

436. Have SAP Business One project team accountabilities & responsibilities been clearly defined?

437. Is your organization certified as a supplier, wholesaler and/or regular dealer?

438. Are parking lot items captured?

439. Pareto diagrams, statistical sampling, flow charting or trend analysis used quality monitoring?

440. Have key stakeholders been identified?

441. Were SAP Business One project team members involved in detailed estimating and scheduling?

442. Are actuals compared against estimates to analyze and correct variances?

443. Are risk triggers captured?

444. Are schedule deliverables actually delivered?

445. Scope of work – What is the scope of work for each of the planned contracts?

446. Schedule contingency – how will the schedule

contingency be administrated?

447. Has a sponsor been identified?

448. Are quality inspections and review activities listed in the SAP Business One project schedule(s)?

449. Are change requests logged and managed?

450. Has the SAP Business One project scope been baselined?

451. Are all payments made according to the contract(s)?

452. Forecasts – how will the cost to complete the SAP Business One project be forecast?

453. Are the appropriate IT resources adequate to meet planned commitments?

454. Owner, contractor, and subcontractors?

2.21 Activity Cost Estimates: SAP Business One

455. Is there anything unique in this SAP Business One projects scope statement that will affect resources?

456. What are the audit requirements?

457. Why do you manage cost?

458. Were you satisfied with the work?

459. How quickly can the task be done with the skills available?

460. Which contract type places the most risk on the seller?

461. One way to define activities is to consider how organization employees describe jobs to families and friends. You basically want to know, What do you do?

462. What is your organizations history in doing similar tasks?

463. What is the activity inventory?

464. What communication items need improvement?

465. What do you want to know about the stay to know if costs were inappropriately high or low?

466. Will you use any tools, such as SAP Business One

project management software, to assist in capturing Earned Value metrics?

467. What were things that you need to improve?

468. Can you change your activities?

469. What makes a good activity description?

470. Measurable - are the targets measurable?

471. Specific - is the objective clear in terms of what, how, when, and where the situation will be changed?

472. What skill level is required to do the job?

2.22 Cost Estimating Worksheet: SAP Business One

473. What is the purpose of estimating?

474. What costs are to be estimated?

475. Is it feasible to establish a control group arrangement?

476. Is the SAP Business One project responsive to community need?

477. Can a trend be established from historical performance data on the selected measure and are the criteria for using trend analysis or forecasting methods met?

478. How will the results be shared and to whom?

479. Ask: are others positioned to know, are others credible, and will others cooperate?

480. Who is best positioned to know and assist in identifying corresponding factors?

481. Does the SAP Business One project provide innovative ways for stakeholders to overcome obstacles or deliver better outcomes?

482. Identify the timeframe necessary to monitor progress and collect data to determine how the selected measure has changed?

483. What additional SAP Business One project(s) could be initiated as a result of this SAP Business One project?

484. What will others want?

485. What happens to any remaining funds not used?

486. Will the SAP Business One project collaborate with the local community and leverage resources?

487. What is the estimated labor cost today based upon this information?

488. What can be included?

2.23 Cost Baseline: SAP Business One

489. Are you meeting with your team regularly?

490. What weaknesses do you have?

491. Have all approved changes to the schedule baseline been identified and impact on the SAP Business One project documented?

492. Have all the product or service deliverables been accepted by the customer?

493. Should a more thorough impact analysis be conducted?

494. SAP Business One project goals -should others be reconsidered?

495. Does it impact schedule, cost, quality?

496. If you sold 10x widgets on a day, what would the affect on profits be?

497. Is request in line with priorities?

498. Will the SAP Business One project fail if the change request is not executed?

499. Where do changes come from?

500. Eac -estimate at completion, what is the total job expected to cost?

501. What strengths do you have?

502. How will cost estimates be used?

503. Definition of done can be traced back to the definitions of what are you providing to the customer in terms of deliverables?

504. Is there anything you need from upper management in order to be successful?

505. Is there anything unique in this SAP Business One projects scope statement that will affect resources?

506. What deliverables come first?

507. What is the consequence?

2.24 Quality Management Plan: SAP Business One

508. Sampling part of task?

509. How long do you retain data?

510. How does your organization establish and maintain customer relationships?

511. Have all necessary approvals been obtained?

512. Results Available?

513. Is this a Requirement?

514. Do trained quality assurance auditors conduct the audits as defined in the Quality Management Plan and scheduled by the SAP Business One project manager?

515. What is the audience for the data?

516. What would you gain if you spent time working to improve this process?

517. How are changes to procedures made?

518. Was trending evident between reviews?

519. How does the material compare to a regulatory threshold?

520. What is the Difference Between a QMP and QAPP?

521. Who do you send data to?

522. Have all involved stakeholders and work groups committed to the SAP Business One project?

523. How does your organization decide what to measure?

524. How is equipment calibrated?

525. You know what your customers expectations are regarding this process?

526. Does the program conduct field testing?

527. How do you ensure that your sampling methods and procedures meet your data quality objectives?

2.25 Quality Metrics: SAP Business One

528. Do you stratify metrics by product or site?

529. What do you measure?

530. What are your organizations expectations for its quality SAP Business One project?

531. Is a risk containment plan in place?

532. Who notifies stakeholders of normal and abnormal results?

533. Who is willing to lead?

534. Have alternatives been defined in the event that failure occurs?

535. What if the biggest risk to your business were the already stated people who do not complain?

536. Are quality metrics defined?

537. How exactly do you define when differences exist?

538. Do the operators focus on determining; is there anything you need to worry about?

539. What group is empowered to define quality requirements?

540. Have risk areas been identified?

541. What metrics are important and most beneficial to measure?

542. How do you calculate such metrics?

543. How does one achieve stability?

544. How do you know if everyone is trying to improve the right things?

545. Where is quality now?

546. Is there alignment within your organization on definitions?

547. If the defect rate during testing is substantially higher than that of the previous release (or a similar product), then ask: Did you plan for and actually improve testing effectiveness?

2.26 Process Improvement Plan: SAP Business One

548. What is quality and how will you ensure it?

549. Have the supporting tools been developed or acquired?

550. Who should prepare the process improvement action plan?

551. How do you manage quality?

552. Are you following the quality standards?

553. Has the time line required to move measurement results from the points of collection to databases or users been established?

554. To elicit goal statements, do you ask a question such as, What do you want to achieve?

555. What is the return on investment?

556. Have storage and access mechanisms and procedures been determined?

557. Does your process ensure quality?

558. What is the test-cycle concept?

559. The motive is determined by asking, Why do you want to achieve this goal?

560. Everyone agrees on what process improvement is, right?

561. What lessons have you learned so far?

562. What makes people good SPI coaches?

563. Are you meeting the quality standards?

564. Are you making progress on your improvement plan?

565. Are you making progress on the goals?

566. Have the frequency of collection and the points in the process where measurements will be made been determined?

567. Where do you want to be?

2.27 Responsibility Assignment Matrix: SAP Business One

568. Changes in the current direct and SAP Business One projected base?

569. Authorization to proceed with all authorized work?

570. If a role has only Signing-off, or only Communicating responsibility and has no Performing, Accountable, or Monitoring responsibility, is it necessary?

571. Evaluate the impact of schedule changes, work around, etc?

572. Are others working on the right things?

573. What does wbs accomplish?

574. Changes in the nature of the overhead requirements?

575. How do you assist them to be as productive as possible?

576. Are the wbs and organizational levels for application of the SAP Business One projected overhead costs identified?

577. Does the contractor use objective results, design reviews and tests to trace schedule performance?

578. Who is responsible for work and budgets for each wbs?

579. Is data disseminated to the contractors management timely, accurate, and usable?

580. Are people afraid to let you know when others are under allocated?

581. Contract line items and end items?

582. Too many is: do all the identified roles need to be routinely informed or only in exceptional circumstances?

583. Direct labor dollars and/or hours?

2.28 Roles and Responsibilities: SAP Business One

584. What specific behaviors did you observe?

585. Implementation of actions: Who are the responsible units?

586. Do you take the time to clearly define roles and responsibilities on SAP Business One project tasks?

587. How well did the SAP Business One project Team understand the expectations of specific roles and responsibilities?

588. What is working well?

589. What should you do now to prepare yourself for a promotion, increased responsibilities or a different job?

590. Are the quality assurance functions and related roles and responsibilities clearly defined?

591. Was the expectation clearly communicated?

592. Are governance roles and responsibilities documented?

593. What should you do now to prepare for your career 5+ years from now?

594. Is there a training program in place for

stakeholders covering expectations, roles and responsibilities and any addition knowledge others need to be good stakeholders?

595. What areas would you highlight for changes or improvements?

596. Are your budgets supportive of a culture of quality data?

597. Authority: what areas/SAP Business One projects in your work do you have the authority to decide upon and act on the already stated decisions?

598. What expectations were NOT met?

599. Who is responsible for implementation activities and where will the functions, roles and responsibilities be defined?

600. What should you highlight for improvement?

601. Once the responsibilities are defined for the SAP Business One project, have the deliverables, roles and responsibilities been clearly communicated to every participant?

2.29 Human Resource Management Plan: SAP Business One

602. Do SAP Business One project teams & team members report on status / activities / progress?

603. Is the SAP Business One project schedule available for all SAP Business One project team members to review?

604. Where is your organization headed?

605. Cost / benefit analysis?

606. Does the resource management plan include a personnel development plan?

607. Are the right people being attracted and retained to meet the future challenges?

608. Do SAP Business One project managers participating in the SAP Business One project know the SAP Business One projects true status first hand?

609. Are procurement deliverables arriving on time and to specification?

610. Was the scope definition used in task sequencing?

611. Are adequate resources provided for the quality assurance function?

612. Are all resource assumptions documented?

613. What areas does the group agree are the biggest success on the SAP Business One project?

614. Is SAP Business One project status reviewed with the steering and executive teams at appropriate intervals?

615. Have adequate resources been provided by management to ensure SAP Business One project success?

616. Is your organization heading towards expansion, outsourcing of certain talents or making cut-backs to save money?

617. Does the detailed work plan match the complexity of tasks with the capabilities of personnel?

2.30 Communications Management Plan: SAP Business One

618. Which stakeholders can influence others?

619. How much time does it take to do it?

620. Who needs to know and how much?

621. How will the person responsible for executing the communication item be notified?

622. Who is involved as you identify stakeholders?

623. Where do team members get information?

624. What are the interrelationships?

625. What approaches do you use?

626. Are there common objectives between the team and the stakeholder?

627. How is this initiative related to other portfolios, programs, or SAP Business One projects?

628. What does the stakeholder need from the team?

629. Do you prepare stakeholder engagement plans?

630. What is the stakeholders level of authority?

631. Are others part of the communications

management plan?

632. Why manage stakeholders?

633. Who were proponents/opponents?

634. How do you manage communications?

635. Will messages be directly related to the release strategy or phases of the SAP Business One project?

636. Who is the stakeholder?

2.31 Risk Management Plan: SAP Business One

637. What is the impact to the SAP Business One project if the item is not resolved in a timely fashion?

638. Can you stabilize dynamic risk factors?

639. Why is product liability a serious issue?

640. What other risks are created by choosing an avoidance strategy?

641. Are SAP Business One project requirements stable?

642. Which risks should get the attention?

643. Is the customer willing to participate in reviews?

644. Are testing tools available and suitable?

645. Are requirements fully understood by the software engineering team and customers?

646. How do you manage SAP Business One project Risk?

647. Is this an issue, action item, question or a risk?

648. Why do you want risk management?

649. Do you manage the process through use of

metrics?

650. Are there alternative opinions/solutions/ processes you should explore?

651. Which is an input to the risk management process?

652. My SAP Business One project leader has suddenly left your organization, what do you do?

653. Do end-users have realistic expectations?

654. How quickly does this item need to be resolved?

655. Do requirements put excessive performance constraints on the product?

656. Are the software tools integrated with each other?

2.32 Risk Register: SAP Business One

657. How is a Community Risk Register created?

658. What is a Community Risk Register?

659. Financial risk -can your organization afford to undertake the SAP Business One project?

660. Are there any gaps in the evidence?

661. Are there other alternative controls that could be implemented?

662. What is the reason for current performance gaps and do the risks and opportunities identified previously account for this?

663. What risks might negatively or positively affect achieving the SAP Business One project objectives?

664. Who needs to know about this?

665. What evidence do you have to justify the likelihood score of the risk (audit, incident report, claim, complaints, inspection, internal review)?

666. How are risks graded?

667. Who is going to do it?

668. Risk categories: what are the main categories of risks that should be addressed on this SAP Business One project?

669. Are implemented controls working as others should?

670. Technology risk -is the SAP Business One project technically feasible?

671. What are the major risks facing the SAP Business One project?

672. How often will the Risk Management Plan and Risk Register be formally reviewed, and by whom?

673. Is further information required before making a decision?

674. When will it happen?

675. People risk -are people with appropriate skills available to help complete the SAP Business One project?

2.33 Probability and Impact Assessment: SAP Business One

676. How risk averse are you?

677. Is security a central objective?

678. To what extent is the chosen technology maturing?

679. Your customers business requirements have suddenly shifted because of a new regulatory statute, what now?

680. How do you define a risk?

681. What are the channels available for distribution to the customer?

682. What is the likelihood?

683. Are there new risks that mitigation strategies might introduce?

684. What is the SAP Business One project managers level of commitment and professionalism?

685. How solid is the SAP Business One projection of competitive reaction?

686. Have customers been involved fully in the definition of requirements?

687. What are the tools and techniques used in managing the challenges faced?

688. Should the risk be taken at all?

689. What would be the effect of slippage?

690. Does the customer have a solid idea of what is required?

691. What are the risks involved in appointing external agencies to manage the SAP Business One project?

692. How are the local factors going to affect the absorption?

693. What should be done with non-critical risks?

694. How are you working with risks?

2.34 Probability and Impact Matrix: SAP Business One

695. Which should be probably done NEXT?

696. How much risk do others need to take?

697. What are its business ethics?

698. Do you have specific methods that you use for each phase of the process?

699. What can go wrong?

700. Can you handle the investment risk?

701. Do you have a consistent repeatable process that is actually used?

702. Do requirements demand the use of new analysis, design, or testing methods?

703. What will be the environmental impact of the SAP Business One project?

704. How would you define a risk?

705. Why do you need to manage SAP Business One project Risk?

706. Premium on reliability of product?

707. What are the chances the event will occur?

708. Which role do you have in the SAP Business One project?

709. How well is the risk understood?

710. How is the SAP Business One project going to be managed?

2.35 Risk Data Sheet: SAP Business One

711. What are the main opportunities available to you that you should grab while you can?

712. What can happen?

713. What actions can be taken to eliminate or remove risk?

714. What are you weak at and therefore need to do better?

715. Who has a vested interest in how you perform as your organization (our stakeholders)?

716. Risk of what?

717. Are new hazards created?

718. What are you trying to achieve (Objectives)?

719. During work activities could hazards exist?

720. How reliable is the data source?

721. What do you know?

722. How do you handle product safely?

723. What was measured?

724. What is the likelihood of it happening?

725. Type of risk identified?

726. Has a sensitivity analysis been carried out?

727. Do effective diagnostic tests exist?

728. Will revised controls lead to tolerable risk levels?

729. What can you do?

730. What do people affected think about the need for, and practicality of preventive measures?

2.36 Procurement Management Plan: SAP Business One

731. Is there a formal set of procedures supporting Stakeholder Management?

732. Has the SAP Business One project scope been baselined?

733. Is there a procurement management plan in place?

734. Are action items captured and managed?

735. Are meeting minutes captured and sent out after meetings?

736. Have all team members been part of identifying risks?

737. Is a stakeholder management plan in place that covers topics?

738. Are the budget estimates reasonable?

739. Are corrective actions and variances reported?

740. Is there any form of automated support for Issues Management?

741. Staffing Requirements?

742. What is the last item a SAP Business One project

manager must do to finalize SAP Business One project close-out?

743. If standardized procurement documents are needed, where can others be found?

744. Are changes in deliverable commitments agreed to by all affected groups & individuals?

2.37 Source Selection Criteria: SAP Business One

745. Is experience evaluated?

746. What are the limitations on pre-competitive range communications?

747. If the costs are normalized, please account for how the normalization is conducted. Is a cost realism analysis used?

748. What are the most common types of rating systems?

749. Is there collaboration among your evaluators?

750. In order of importance, which evaluation criteria are the most critical to the determination of your overall rating?

751. What are the guidelines regarding award without considerations?

752. What information is to be provided and when should it be provided?

753. Are evaluators ready to begin this task?

754. How and when do you enter into SAP Business One project Procurement Management?

755. How are clarifications and communications

appropriately used?

756. When is it appropriate to issue a Draft Request for Proposal (DRFP)?

757. What should be the contracting officers strategy?

758. In which phase of the acquisition process cycle does source qualifications reside?

759. Does your documentation identify why the team concurs or differs with reported performance from past performance report (CPARs, questionnaire responses, etc.)?

760. When is it appropriate to issue a DRFP?

761. How do you ensure an integrated assessment of proposals?

762. What should preproposal conferences accomplish?

763. What common questions or problems are associated with debriefings?

2.38 Stakeholder Management Plan: SAP Business One

764. What procedures will be utilised to ensure effective monitoring of SAP Business One project progress?

765. Have the procedures for identifying budget variances been followed?

766. Were the budget estimates reasonable?

767. Is the communication plan being followed?

768. Have SAP Business One project team accountabilities & responsibilities been clearly defined?

769. Why would you develop a SAP Business One project Business Plan?

770. What action will be taken once reports have been received?

771. Have all documents been archived in a SAP Business One project repository for each release?

772. Are meeting minutes captured and sent out after the meeting?

773. Have adequate resources been provided by management to ensure SAP Business One project success?

774. Who will perform the review(s)?

775. Has a resource management plan been created?

776. Can the requirements be traced to the appropriate components of the solution, as well as test scripts?

777. Are there procedures in place to effectively manage interdependencies with other SAP Business One projects / systems?

778. Quality assurance overheads?

779. Are mitigation strategies identified?

2.39 Change Management Plan: SAP Business One

780. What provokes organizational change?

781. What prerequisite knowledge or training is required?

782. Is there a software application relevant to this deliverable?

783. Who will do the training?

784. How will you deal with anger about the restricting of communications due to confidentiality considerations?

785. What work practices will be affected?

786. Are work location changes required?

787. What is the negative impact of communicating too soon or too late?

788. How will the stakeholders share information and transfer knowledge?

789. What method and medium would you use to announce a message?

790. What does a resilient organization look like?

791. How badly can information be misinterpreted?

792. Would you need to tailor a special message for each segment of the audience?

793. Different application of an existing process?

794. Has the training provider been established?

795. What relationships will change?

796. When does it make sense to customize?

797. What is the most cynical response it can receive?

798. Identify the current level of skills and knowledge and behaviours of the group that will be impacted on. What prerequisite knowledge do corresponding groups need?

799. Will you need new processes?

3.0 Executing Process Group: SAP Business One

800. Why is it important to determine activity sequencing on SAP Business One projects?

801. What are the challenges SAP Business One project teams face?

802. Is activity definition the first process involved in SAP Business One project time management?

803. How will you avoid scope creep?

804. How many different communication channels does the SAP Business One project team have?

805. What type of information goes in the quality assurance plan?

806. What areas does the group agree are the biggest success on the SAP Business One project?

807. What are deliverables of your SAP Business One project?

808. How do you prevent staff are just doing busywork to pass the time?

809. Do the partners have sufficient financial capacity to keep up the benefits produced by the programme?

810. How well did the team follow the chosen

processes?

811. What are the SAP Business One project management deliverables of each process group?

812. How is SAP Business One project performance information created and distributed?

813. Would you rate yourself as being risk-averse, risk-neutral, or risk-seeking?

814. If a risk event occurs, what will you do?

815. How will professionals learn what is expected from them what the deliverables are?

816. How can you use Microsoft SAP Business One project and Excel to assist in SAP Business One project risk management?

3.1 Team Member Status Report: SAP Business One

817. How can you make it practical?

818. Why is it to be done?

819. How much risk is involved?

820. Is there evidence that staff is taking a more professional approach toward management of your organizations SAP Business One projects?

821. Are the products of your organizations SAP Business One projects meeting customers objectives?

822. Are your organizations SAP Business One projects more successful over time?

823. Does your organization have the means (staff, money, contract, etc.) to produce or to acquire the product, good, or service?

824. The problem with Reward & Recognition Programs is that the truly deserving people all too often get left out. How can you make it practical?

825. What specific interest groups do you have in place?

826. How it is to be done?

827. How will resource planning be done?

828. When a teams productivity and success depend on collaboration and the efficient flow of information, what generally fails them?

829. Are the attitudes of staff regarding SAP Business One project work improving?

830. Does every department have to have a SAP Business One project Manager on staff?

831. Does the product, good, or service already exist within your organization?

832. Do you have an Enterprise SAP Business One project Management Office (EPMO)?

833. Will the staff do training or is that done by a third party?

834. What is to be done?

835. How does this product, good, or service meet the needs of the SAP Business One project and your organization as a whole?

3.2 Change Request: SAP Business One

836. Does the schedule include SAP Business One project management time and change request analysis time?

837. How is the change documented (format, content, storage)?

838. What is the change request log?

839. How many lines of code must be changed to implement the change?

840. What should be regulated in a change control operating instruction?

841. Will new change requests be acknowledged in a timely manner?

842. How do you get changes (code) out in a timely manner?

843. Will all change requests and current status be logged?

844. Who is included in the change control team?

845. How are changes requested (forms, method of communication)?

846. Why were your requested changes rejected or

not made?

847. Can static requirements change attributes like the size of the change be used to predict reliability in execution?

848. Which requirements attributes affect the risk to reliability the most?

849. What can be filed?

850. How can changes be graded?

851. What is the function of the change control committee?

852. What are the basic mechanics of the Change Advisory Board (CAB)?

853. Will there be a change request form in use?

854. How is quality being addressed on the SAP Business One project?

3.3 Change Log: SAP Business One

855. How does this change affect scope?

856. Is the submitted change a new change or a modification of a previously approved change?

857. Does the suggested change request represent a desired enhancement to the products functionality?

858. Is the change request within SAP Business One project scope?

859. Will the SAP Business One project fail if the change request is not executed?

860. Do the described changes impact on the integrity or security of the system?

861. When was the request submitted?

862. Is the change request open, closed or pending?

863. Is the change backward compatible without limitations?

864. Is the requested change request a result of changes in other SAP Business One project(s)?

865. How does this change affect the timeline of the schedule?

866. When was the request approved?

867. Who initiated the change request?

868. How does this relate to the standards developed for specific business processes?

869. Is this a mandatory replacement?

870. Does the suggested change request seem to represent a necessary enhancement to the product?

3.4 Decision Log: SAP Business One

871. How effective is maintaining the log at facilitating organizational learning?

872. Does anything need to be adjusted?

873. Decision-making process; how will the team make decisions?

874. Meeting purpose; why does this team meet?

875. Is everything working as expected?

876. What makes you different or better than others companies selling the same thing?

877. What alternatives/risks were considered?

878. How does the use a Decision Support System influence the strategies/tactics or costs?

879. Which variables make a critical difference?

880. How do you know when you are achieving it?

881. Is your opponent open to a non-traditional workflow, or will it likely challenge anything you do?

882. What is your overall strategy for quality control / quality assurance procedures?

883. At what point in time does loss become unacceptable?

884. What are the cost implications?

885. What was the rationale for the decision?

886. Do strategies and tactics aimed at less than full control reduce the costs of management or simply shift the cost burden?

887. Linked to original objective?

888. Behaviors; what are guidelines that the team has identified that will assist them with getting the most out of team meetings?

889. What eDiscovery problem or issue did your organization set out to fix or make better?

890. Who will be given a copy of this document and where will it be kept?

3.5 Quality Audit: SAP Business One

891. Do all staff have the necessary authority and resources to deliver what is expected of them?

892. What is the collective experience of the team to be assigned to an audit?

893. Is there a written procedure for receiving materials?

894. How does your organization know that its relationships with industry and employers are appropriately effective and constructive?

895. How does your organization know that its range of activities are being reviewed as rigorously and constructively as they could be?

896. Is there any content that may be legally actionable?

897. Are adequate and conveniently located toilet facilities available for use by the employees?

898. Does your organization have set of goals, objectives, strategies and targets that are clearly understood by the Board and staff?

899. How is the Strategic Plan (and other plans) reviewed and revised?

900. How does the organization know that its industry and community engagement planning and

management systems are appropriately effective and constructive in enabling relationships with key stakeholder groups?

901. How do staff know if they are doing a good job?

902. Is there a written corporate quality policy?

903. How does your organization know that its staff have appropriate access to a fair and effective grievance process?

904. How does your organization know that the support for its staff is appropriately effective and constructive?

905. How does your organization know that its relationships with other relevant organizations are appropriately effective and constructive?

906. How are you auditing your organizations compliance with regulations?

907. How does your organization know that the research supervision provided to its staff is appropriately effective and constructive?

908. Are the review comments incorporated?

909. How does your organization know that its systems for communicating with and among staff are appropriately effective and constructive?

910. How does your organization know that its staff embody the core knowledge, skills and characteristics for which it wishes to be recognized?

3.6 Team Directory: SAP Business One

911. How does the team resolve conflicts and ensure tasks are completed?

912. Who are the Team Members?

913. Process decisions: are there any statutory or regulatory issues relevant to the timely execution of work?

914. Decisions: what could be done better to improve the quality of the constructed product?

915. Timing: when do the effects of communication take place?

916. What are you going to deliver or accomplish?

917. Who is the Sponsor?

918. Process decisions: are all start-up, turn over and close out requirements of the contract satisfied?

919. Process decisions: is work progressing on schedule and per contract requirements?

920. Have you decided when to celebrate the SAP Business One projects completion date?

921. Do purchase specifications and configurations match requirements?

922. Is construction on schedule?

923. Why is the work necessary?

924. Process decisions: are contractors adequately prosecuting the work?

925. Contract requirements complied with?

926. Does a SAP Business One project team directory list all resources assigned to the SAP Business One project?

927. Who will report SAP Business One project status to all stakeholders?

928. How and in what format should information be presented?

3.7 Team Operating Agreement: SAP Business One

929. Do you vary your voice pace, tone and pitch to engage participants and gain involvement?

930. What is culture?

931. Are there influences outside the team that may affect performance, and if so, have you identified and addressed them?

932. Do you send out the agenda and meeting materials in advance?

933. What are the current caseload numbers in the unit?

934. To whom do you deliver your services?

935. What is your unique contribution to your organization?

936. Did you draft the meeting agenda?

937. Do you use a parking lot for any items that are important and outside of the agenda?

938. Do you solicit member feedback about meetings and what would make them better?

939. What are the safety issues/risks that need to be addressed and/or that the team needs to consider?

940. Did you determine the technology methods that best match the messages to be communicated?

941. Have you established procedures that team members can follow to work effectively together, such as a team operating agreement?

942. What is group supervision?

943. Why does your organization want to participate in teaming?

944. Seconds for members to respond?

945. Do team members need to frequently communicate as a full group to make timely decisions?

946. Do you listen for voice tone and word choice to understand the meaning behind words?

947. Do you upload presentation materials in advance and test the technology?

3.8 Team Performance Assessment: SAP Business One

948. Individual task proficiency and team process behavior: what is important for team functioning?

949. If you have criticized someones work for method variance in your role as reviewer, what was the circumstance?

950. To what degree can team members vigorously define the teams purpose in considerations with others who are not part of the functioning team?

951. To what degree is the team cognizant of small wins to be celebrated along the way?

952. To what degree can the team ensure that all members are individually and jointly accountable for the teams purpose, goals, approach, and work-products?

953. To what degree do team members frequently explore the teams purpose and its implications?

954. To what degree is there a sense that only the team can succeed?

955. To what degree will new and supplemental skills be introduced as the need is recognized?

956. Delaying market entry: how long is too long?

957. To what degree are the teams goals and objectives clear, simple, and measurable?

958. To what degree do team members understand one anothers roles and skills?

959. Can team performance be reliably measured in simulator and live exercises using the same assessment tool?

960. To what degree can all members engage in open and interactive considerations?

961. To what degree will the team adopt a concrete, clearly understood, and agreed-upon approach that will result in achievement of the teams goals?

962. To what degree are the skill areas critical to team performance present?

963. How do you recognize and praise members for contributions?

964. Lack of method variance in self-reported affect and perceptions at work: Reality or artifact?

965. To what degree will the team ensure that all members equitably share the work essential to the success of the team?

966. To what degree do team members feel that the purpose of the team is important, if not exciting?

967. To what degree does the teams work approach provide opportunity for members to engage in open interaction?

3.9 Team Member Performance Assessment: SAP Business One

968. What is the Business Management Oversight Process?

969. To what degree do the goals specify concrete team work products?

970. Who is responsible?

971. What happens if a team member receives a Rating of Unsatisfactory?

972. How was the determination made for which training platforms would be used (i.e., media selection)?

973. How will they be formed?

974. Why were corresponding selected?

975. Which training platform formats (i.e., mobile, virtual, videogame-based) were implemented in your effort(s)?

976. In what areas would you like to concentrate your knowledge and resources?

977. Who should attend?

978. To what degree can the team measure progress against specific goals?

979. How do you determine which data are the most important to use, analyze, or review?

980. To what degree are the relative importance and priority of the goals clear to all team members?

981. To what extent are systems and applications (e.g., game engine, mobile device platform) utilized?

982. What future plans (e.g., modifications) do you have for your program?

983. How accurately is your plan implemented?

984. What were the challenges that resulted for training and assessment?

3.10 Issue Log: SAP Business One

985. Are you constantly rushing from meeting to meeting?

986. How often do you engage with stakeholders?

987. Are there potential barriers between the team and the stakeholder?

988. How is this initiative related to other portfolios, programs, or SAP Business One projects?

989. How do you reply to this question; you am new here and managing this major program. How do you suggest you build your network?

990. Is access to the Issue Log controlled?

991. Are they needed?

992. Why not more evaluators?

993. Why do you manage communications?

994. Who is the issue assigned to?

995. What are the typical contents?

996. Who do you turn to if you have questions?

997. What help do you and your team need from the stakeholders?

998. What is the stakeholders political influence?

999. What effort will a change need?

4.0 Monitoring and Controlling Process Group: SAP Business One

1000. Do clients benefit (change) from the services?

1001. What areas does the group agree are the biggest success on the SAP Business One project?

1002. Key stakeholders to work with. How many potential communications channels exist on the SAP Business One project?

1003. Contingency planning. if a risk event occurs, what will you do?

1004. How is Agile SAP Business One project Management done?

1005. Is there sufficient funding available for this?

1006. Propriety: who needs to be involved in the evaluation to be ethical?

1007. What resources (both financial and non-financial) are available/needed?

1008. Where is the Risk in the SAP Business One project?

1009. How do you monitor progress?

1010. What good practices or successful experiences or transferable examples have been identified?

1011. Change, where should you look for problems?

1012. When will the SAP Business One project be done?

1013. Is there undesirable impact on staff or resources?

1014. How is agile portfolio management done?

1015. Overall, how does the program function to serve the clients?

1016. How can you monitor progress?

1017. Is it what was agreed upon?

4.1 Project Performance Report: SAP Business One

1018. To what degree do all members feel responsible for all agreed-upon measures?

1019. To what degree does the information network communicate information relevant to the task?

1020. What is the degree to which rules govern information exchange between groups?

1021. What is the PRS?

1022. To what degree does the task meet individual needs?

1023. To what degree does the funding match the requirement?

1024. To what degree does the team possess adequate membership to achieve its ends?

1025. What degree are the relative importance and priority of the goals clear to all team members?

1026. To what degree does the information network provide individuals with the information they require?

1027. To what degree can team members frequently and easily communicate with one another?

1028. To what degree are the tasks requirements

reflected in the flow and storage of information?

1029. To what degree do team members articulate the teams work approach?

1030. How is the data used?

1031. To what degree is there centralized control of information sharing?

4.2 Variance Analysis: SAP Business One

1032. Are work packages assigned to performing organizations?

1033. What types of services and expense are shared between business segments?

1034. How does your organization allocate the cost of shared expenses and services?

1035. Are overhead costs budgets established on a basis consistent with the anticipated direct business base?

1036. How are material, labor, and overhead variances calculated and recorded?

1037. What business event causes fluctuations?

1038. Are meaningful indicators identified for use in measuring the status of cost and schedule performance?

1039. There are detailed schedules which support control account and work package start and completion dates/events?

1040. Did your organization lose existing customers and/or gain new customers?

1041. Are material costs reported within the same

period as that in which BCWP is earned for that material?

1042. Why do variances exist?

1043. What business event caused the fluctuation?

1044. Is the entire contract planned in time-phased control accounts to the extent practicable?

1045. Is budgeted cost for work performed calculated in a manner consistent with the way work is planned?

1046. Are data elements reconcilable between internal summary reports and reports forwarded to the stakeholders?

1047. What should management do?

1048. Are all budgets assigned to control accounts?

1049. Is cost and schedule performance measurement done in a consistent, systematic manner?

4.3 Earned Value Status: SAP Business One

1050. How does this compare with other SAP Business One projects?

1051. If earned value management (EVM) is so good in determining the true status of a SAP Business One project and SAP Business One project its completion, why is it that hardly any one uses it in information systems related SAP Business One projects?

1052. Where is evidence-based earned value in your organization reported?

1053. Validation is a process of ensuring that the developed system will actually achieve the stakeholders desired outcomes; Are you building the right product? What do you validate?

1054. How much is it going to cost by the finish?

1055. What is the unit of forecast value?

1056. Earned value can be used in almost any SAP Business One project situation and in almost any SAP Business One project environment. it may be used on large SAP Business One projects, medium sized SAP Business One projects, tiny SAP Business One projects (in cut-down form), complex and simple SAP Business One projects and in any market sector. some people, of course, know all about earned value, they have used it for years - but perhaps not as effectively as they could have?

1057. When is it going to finish?

1058. Verification is a process of ensuring that the developed system satisfies the stakeholders agreements and specifications; Are you building the product right? What do you verify?

1059. Where are your problem areas?

1060. Are you hitting your SAP Business One projects targets?

4.4 Risk Audit: SAP Business One

1061. Who is responsible for what?

1062. Assessing risk with analytical procedures: do systemsthinking tools help auditors focus on diagnostic patterns?

1063. What risk does not having unique identification present?

1064. What are the outcomes you are looking for?

1065. Are team members trained in the use of the tools?

1066. Is your organization an exempt employer for payroll tax purposes?

1067. How are risk appetites expressed?

1068. How do you compare to other jurisdictions when managing the risk of ....?

1069. What expertise do auditors need to generate effective business-level risk assessments, and to what extent do auditors currently possess the already stated attributes?

1070. What resources are needed to achieve program results?

1071. Whence the business risk audit?

1072. Does your organization have a social media policy and procedure?

1073. Does your board meet regularly and document all decisions and actions?

1074. What are the strategic implications with clients when auditors focus audit resources based on business-level risks?

1075. When your organization is entering into a major contract, does it seek legal advice?

1076. Do industry specialists and business risk auditors enhance audit reporting accuracy?

1077. Is an annual audit required and conducted of your financial records?

1078. Has an event time line been developed?

4.5 Contractor Status Report: SAP Business One

1079. If applicable; describe your standard schedule for new software version releases. Are new software version releases included in the standard maintenance plan?

1080. Describe how often regular updates are made to the proposed solution. Are corresponding regular updates included in the standard maintenance plan?

1081. How does the proposed individual meet each requirement?

1082. How is risk transferred?

1083. What was the actual budget or estimated cost for your organizations services?

1084. Are there contractual transfer concerns?

1085. Who can list a SAP Business One project as organization experience, your organization or a previous employee of your organization?

1086. What was the overall budget or estimated cost?

1087. What is the average response time for answering a support call?

1088. How long have you been using the services?

1089. What was the final actual cost?

1090. What was the budget or estimated cost for your organizations services?

1091. What process manages the contracts?

1092. What are the minimum and optimal bandwidth requirements for the proposed solution?

4.6 Formal Acceptance: SAP Business One

1093. Do you buy-in installation services?

1094. What is the Acceptance Management Process?

1095. Was the client satisfied with the SAP Business One project results?

1096. Did the SAP Business One project achieve its MOV?

1097. Who supplies data?

1098. Do you perform formal acceptance or burn-in tests?

1099. What features, practices, and processes proved to be strengths or weaknesses?

1100. Is formal acceptance of the SAP Business One project product documented and distributed?

1101. Have all comments been addressed?

1102. Was the SAP Business One project work done on time, within budget, and according to specification?

1103. What are the requirements against which to test, Who will execute?

1104. How does your team plan to obtain formal

acceptance on your SAP Business One project?

1105. General estimate of the costs and times to complete the SAP Business One project?

1106. Did the SAP Business One project manager and team act in a professional and ethical manner?

1107. Who would use it?

1108. Does it do what client said it would?

1109. Was the SAP Business One project goal achieved?

1110. Do you buy pre-configured systems or build your own configuration?

1111. What function(s) does it fill or meet?

1112. What was done right?

5.0 Closing Process Group: SAP Business One

1113. Is this a follow-on to a previous SAP Business One project?

1114. Did you do what you said you were going to do?

1115. Is this an updated SAP Business One project Proposal Document?

1116. How critical is the SAP Business One project success to the success of your organization?

1117. Were risks identified and mitigated?

1118. Mitigate. what will you do to minimize the impact should a risk event occur?

1119. What is an Encumbrance?

1120. Based on your SAP Business One project communication management plan, what worked well?

1121. Did the SAP Business One project team have the right skills?

1122. How well did the chosen processes fit the needs of the SAP Business One project?

1123. What areas were overlooked on this SAP Business One project?

1124. What could be done to improve the process?

1125. Was the schedule met?

1126. What will you do to minimize the impact should a risk event occur?

1127. What were the desired outcomes?

1128. Did the SAP Business One project management methodology work?

1129. Can the lesson learned be replicated?

1130. How dependent is the SAP Business One project on other SAP Business One projects or work efforts?

5.1 Procurement Audit: SAP Business One

1131. Were any additional works or deliveries admissible without the need for a new procurement procedure?

1132. Are checks used in numeric sequence?

1133. Do all requests for materials, supplies, and services require supervisors authorization?

1134. Is the procurement SAP Business One project efficiently managed?

1135. Are the official minutes written in a clear and concise manner?

1136. Does the procurement function/unit have the ability to negotiate with customers and suppliers?

1137. Was the pre-qualification screening for issue of tender documents done properly and in a fair manner?

1138. Is authorization required to make changes to the purchase order file?

1139. What are your procurement processes with contractors?

1140. Is there a formal program of inservice training for personnel in the business management function?

1141. Were additional works brought about by a cause which had not previously existed?

1142. Were all interested operators allowed the opportunity to participate?

1143. How do you confirm whether the contracted organization supplied the goods or executed the work as per the quality, quantity and price indicated in the contract agreement/ supply order?

1144. Was the expert likely to gain privileged knowledge from his activity which could be advantageous for him in a subsequent competition?

1145. Is the procurement process fully digitalized?

1146. Do you learn from benchmarking your own practices with international standards?

1147. Was the estimation of contract value in accordance with the criteria fixed in the Directive?

1148. Does the strategy include a policy for identifying and training suitable procurement staff?

1149. Has your organization taken a well-grounded decision about the procurement procedure chosen and has it documented the process?

1150. Has an upper limit of cost been fixed?

5.2 Contract Close-Out: SAP Business One

1151. Parties: Authorized?

1152. Was the contract type appropriate?

1153. How does it work?

1154. Have all contracts been completed?

1155. Change in attitude or behavior?

1156. Change in circumstances?

1157. How/when used ?

1158. Why Outsource?

1159. Are the signers the authorized officials?

1160. Have all contracts been closed?

1161. What is capture management?

1162. How is the contracting office notified of the automatic contract close-out?

1163. Have all contract records been included in the SAP Business One project archives?

1164. Has each contract been audited to verify acceptance and delivery?

1165. Parties: who is involved?

1166. Was the contract sufficiently clear so as not to result in numerous disputes and misunderstandings?

1167. Have all acceptance criteria been met prior to final payment to contractors?

1168. What happens to the recipient of services?

1169. Was the contract complete without requiring numerous changes and revisions?

1170. Change in knowledge?

5.3 Project or Phase Close-Out: SAP Business One

1171. What information did each stakeholder need to contribute to the SAP Business One projects success?

1172. What is a Risk?

1173. What is this stakeholder expecting?

1174. Were messages directly related to the release strategy or phases of the SAP Business One project?

1175. Who is responsible for award close-out?

1176. What is the information level of detail required for each stakeholder?

1177. What are the informational communication needs for each stakeholder?

1178. Does the lesson educate others to improve performance?

1179. What could have been improved?

1180. Was the user/client satisfied with the end product?

1181. What stakeholder group needs, expectations, and interests are being met by the SAP Business One project?

1182. What information is each stakeholder group interested in?

1183. Planned remaining costs?

1184. Is the lesson based on actual SAP Business One project experience rather than on independent research?

1185. Planned completion date?

5.4 Lessons Learned: SAP Business One

1186. How extensive is middle management?

1187. Did the team work well together?

1188. Do you have any real problems?

1189. If issue escalation was required, how effectively were issues resolved?

1190. Was the control overhead justified?

1191. Are corrective actions needed?

1192. How useful was the format and content of the SAP Business One project Status Report to you?

1193. Who needs to learn lessons?

1194. What is your organizations performance history?

1195. How much flexibility is there in the funding (e.g., what authorities does the program manager have to change to the specifics of the funding within the overall funding ceiling)?

1196. What was the single greatest success and the single greatest shortcoming or challenge from the SAP Business One projects perspective?

1197. How effective were SAP Business One project audits?

1198. How adequately involved did you feel in SAP Business One project decisions?

1199. How spontaneous are the communications?

1200. Was the purpose of the SAP Business One project, the end products and success criteria clearly defined and agreed at the start?

1201. How much time is required for the task?

1202. How effective was the quality assurance process?

1203. What worked well or did not work well, either for this SAP Business One project or for the SAP Business One project team?

1204. Who managed most of the communication within the SAP Business One project?

1205. Why do you need to measure?

Index

Printed by BoD™in Norderstedt, Germany

9 780655 915355